FOREIGN AFFAIRS

Special Collection

Darkness Invisible

The Hidden Global Costs of Mental Illness

Thomas R. Insel, Pamela Y. Collins, and Steven E. Hyman

STRINGER / COURTESY REUTERS

The hidden epidemic: in a mental hospital in Shanxi Province, China, October 2010

Four years ago, a team of scholars from the Harvard School of Public Health and the World Economic Forum prepared a report on the current and future global economic burden

THOMAS R. INSEL is Director of the National Institute of Mental Health.

PAMELA Y. COLLINS is Director of the Office for Research on Disparities and Global Mental Health at the National Institute of Mental Health.

STEVEN E. HYMAN is Director of the Stanley Center for Psychiatric Research at the Broad Institute of Harvard and MIT.

of disease. Science and medicine have made tremendous progress in combating infectious diseases during the past five decades, and the group noted that noncommunicable diseases, such as heart disease and diabetes, now pose a greater risk than contagious illnesses. In 2010, the report's authors found, noncommunicable diseases caused 63 percent of all deaths around the world, and 80 percent of those fatalities occurred in countries that the World Bank characterizes as low income or middle income. Noncommunicable diseases are partly rooted in lifestyle and diet, and their emergence as a major risk, especially in the developing world, represents the dark side of the economic advances that have also spurred increased longevity, urbanization, and population growth. The scale of the problem is only going to grow: between 2010 and 2030, the report estimated, chronic noncommunicable diseases will reduce global GDP by $46.7 trillion.

These findings reflected a growing consensus among global health experts and economists. But the report did contain one big surprise: it predicted that the largest source of those tremendous future costs would be mental disorders, which the report forecast would account for more than a third of the global economic burden of noncommunicable diseases by 2030. Taken together, the direct economic effects of mental illness (such as spending on care) and the indirect effects (such as lost productivity) already cost the global economy around $2.5 trillion a year. By 2030, the team projected, that amount will increase to around $6 trillion, in constant dollars— more than heart disease and more than cancer, diabetes, and respiratory diseases combined.

These conclusions were dramatic and disturbing. Yet the report had virtually no impact on debates about public health policy, mostly because it did not manage to dislodge persistent and harmful misperceptions about mental illness. In wealthy countries, most people continue to view mental illness as a problem facing individuals and families, rather than as a policy challenge with significant economic and political implications. Meanwhile, in low-income and middle-income countries and within international organizations, officials tend to view mental illness as a "First World problem"; according to that view, worrying about mental health is a luxury that people living in severe poverty or amid violent conflict cannot afford.

In reality, in countries of all levels of wealth and development, mental illness affects almost every aspect of society and the economy. And far from lacking relevance or urgency in poor and war-torn countries, mental illness often contributes to the very dysfunctions that plague such places. Moreover, breakthroughs in therapy and treatment have significantly improved the efficacy—and lowered the cost—of caring for people who suffer from mental illness, even in places that have traditionally lacked access to mental health services. Policymakers, mental health professionals, and advocates for the mentally ill should take advantage of this progress. To do so, they first must change the way people—including they themselves—think about and talk about mental illness.

BRAIN DRAIN

People underestimate the costs and significance of mental illness for many reasons. At the most basic level, policymakers and public health officials tend to view mental illness as fundamentally different from other medical problems. But just like other diseases, mental illnesses are disorders of a bodily organ: the brain. In this respect, they are no different from other noncommunicable diseases.

Most people also do not realize just how common mental disorders are, in part because such illnesses are stigmatized and thus often hidden. The U.S. Department of Health and Human Services estimates that in 2012, 43.7 million Americans over the age of 18 suffered from some kind of mental disorder—18.6 percent of the country's adult population. Nearly ten million of those people, or 4.1 percent of adult Americans, struggled with serious mental illnesses, such as psychotic disorders. Even in the United States, where treatment for such problems is relatively accessible, many people do not seek or receive care until their disorders have become chronic and disabling, a length of time that one recent study found to be 11 years, on average.

Mental disorders are also far more disabling than most people realize, often preventing the afflicted from working, studying, caring for others, producing, and consuming. In a 2012 report on the global economic burden of disease, the World Health Organization noted that mental illnesses and behavioral disorders account for 26 percent of the time lost to disability—more than any other kind of disease.

The impact of mental illnesses is magnified by the fact that such disorders afflict mostly young people, in contrast to other chronic noncommunicable diseases, such as heart disease or cancer, which generally appear later in life. A 2005 study conducted by researchers at Harvard Medical School, the University of Michigan, and the National Institute of Mental Health found that 75 percent of adults suffering from mental illness reported that their symptoms began before they turned 25. The first signs of psychosis in people with schizophrenia typically arrive between the ages of 18 and 23; autism begins to affect people before the age of three. Such early onset explains why mental disorders represent by far the largest source of disability—and hence lost

Losing It
Top Ten Sources of Time Lost to Disability Globally From All Medical Causes, by Percentage

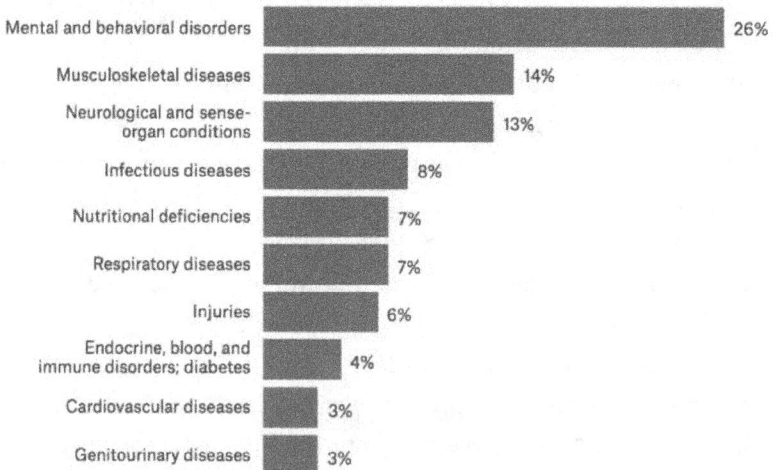

Category	Percentage
Mental and behavioral disorders	26%
Musculoskeletal diseases	14%
Neurological and sense-organ conditions	13%
Infectious diseases	8%
Nutritional deficiencies	7%
Respiratory diseases	7%
Injuries	6%
Endocrine, blood, and immune disorders; diabetes	4%
Cardiovascular diseases	3%
Genitourinary diseases	3%

SOURCE: World Health Organization, 2012.

productivity—for people between the ages of 15 and 44, a crucial period in life during which people transition from school to work, find partners, start families, and build careers.

Another little-understood aspect of mental disorders is that they are not merely disabling; they are deadly. Although many factors lead people to end their own lives, the American Foundation for Suicide Prevention estimates that mental illness plays a role in 90 percent of suicides. The World Health Organization estimates that some 800,000 people commit suicide every year, 75 percent of them in low-income and middle-income countries. Globally, more than twice as many people die from suicide as die from homicide each year, and suicide is the second-largest source of mortality for people aged 15 to 29, topped only by traffic accidents.

Finally, mental disorders act as a gateway to a range of other costly public health problems. Suffering from a mental illness increases one's chances of contracting HIV and of developing heart disease, pulmonary diseases, and diabetes; it also raises one's risk of homelessness, poverty, and institutionalization, including imprisonment—all of which represent further burdens on society.

ATTENTION DEFICIT

Despite these profound costs, mental illness receives surprisingly little attention and resources from governments and international organizations. Globally, annual spending on mental health amounts to less than $2 per person; on average, low-income countries spend less than 25 cents per person. The median amount that countries spend on mental health equals less than three percent of the median amount that they spend on all health care, even though mental illness accounts for over 20 percent of all health-care costs. And the poorer the country, the worse the problem: the World Health Organization estimates that the majority of countries at low and lower-middle levels of income devote less than two percent of their health budgets to treating mental disorders. In such countries, up to 85 percent of people with severe mental illness receive no treatment at all.

Even wealthy countries devote few resources to mental disorders relative to the economic costs they impose. According to the Centre for Economic Performance at the London School of Economics, mental illness costs the British economy around 70 billion pounds in lost productivity and health-care expenditures every year and accounts for 23 percent of the burden that disease places on the United Kingdom, and yet the National Health Service devotes only 13 percent of its expenditures to mental disorders. Nor are international organizations any better attuned to the problem: mental illness went completely unmentioned in the UN's Millennium Development Goals (MDGs), and until recently, most of the major organizations addressing global health and disaster relief paid little attention to the mental health needs of the populations they served.

Owing to this lack of attention and awareness, the costs of treating mental illness often fall outside health-care sectors. In the United States, for instance, most states have almost completely dismantled the system of mental hospitals that once oversaw care for the mentally ill. As a result, Americans with serious mental illness are ten times as likely to be imprisoned as to be in hospitals. In a sense, through welfare programs, social services, and jails and prisons, many countries wind up spending on the effects of mental illness—such as unemployment, homelessness, and incarceration—rather than the underlying causes. In the United States, such indirect costs represent two-thirds of the economic burden of mental health problems—a figure that makes sense considering that 30 percent of the country's chronically homeless and more than 20 percent of the people incarcerated in the United States suffer from a mental disorder.

A FIRST WORLD PROBLEM?

Compared with wealthy countries, low-income and middle-income countries face an even starker challenge when it comes to mental health: a lack of expertise and a shortage of professionals. Residents of wealthy countries enjoy a relatively high concentration of mental health specialists: high-income countries have, on average, nine psychiatrists for every 100,000 people. But almost half of the world's population lives in countries where, on average, there is only one psychiatrist for every 200,000 people; in many African countries, there is only one psychiatrist per every one million people.

In the short term, these numbers are not likely to improve much. But people suffering from mental illness in poorer places could benefit from a relatively new trend in the field: the so-called task-sharing approach, in which professionals train a range of providers—from nurses and social workers to peers and family members—to care for those with mental illness. Controlled trials have already demonstrated the promise this approach holds, even in places with few established mental health resources. In a report published in *The New England Journal of Medicine* in 2013, a team led by Judith Bass, a mental health specialist at Johns Hopkins University, described a controlled trial it had carried out in 2011 involving around 400 women in 16 villages in the Democratic Republic of the Congo who had suffered sexual violence and exhibited symptoms of posttraumatic stress disorder, depression, or anxiety. To test the efficacy of a task-sharing approach to caring for these women, clinical experts from the United States spent five or six days training local women in how to provide cognitive-processing therapy, which focuses on helping people to stop avoiding their problems and instead solve them by changing their behavior.

The local assistants used that approach to treat one set of the victims of violence, 70 percent of whom suffered from symptoms of depression and anxiety disorders before the trial began. A control group of other victims, 83 percent of whom were experiencing such symptoms, received only individual support from the assistants. The results were remarkable: after six months, only ten percent of the women who had received the cognitive-processing therapy still appeared to be suffering from depression or anxiety disorders, compared with 42 percent of those who had received just individual support.

In a 2008 article in *The Lancet*, a team of researchers reported similar results from a controlled trial in rural Pakistan, in which the team trained community health workers to provide a form of treatment resembling cognitive-behavioral therapy to women struggling with prenatal or postpartum depression. Women in 20 rural areas received treatment from the trainees; a control group of women in 20 other areas received care from workers who had not been trained. When the treatment period ended, only 23 percent of the women who had received care from the trained workers showed symptoms consistent with prenatal or postpartum depression, compared with 53 percent of those in the control group.

The results in Congo and Pakistan suggest that task-sharing approaches can produce results equal to or even better than those achieved by such treatments in wealthy countries, where they have been used, to cite one example, to care for U.S. military veterans struggling with posttraumatic stress disorder. And in both Congo and Pakistan, women who received psychotherapeutic treatment showed not only substantial decreases in symptoms but also improvements in overall health and well-being. Nor were they the only beneficiaries: the women who received such treatments in Pakistan were also more likely to obtain crucial vaccines for their children.

PAGING BILL GATES

Another obstacle hindering mental health care in the developing world is that many donors, public health specialists, and government officials believe that mental illness cannot be addressed with the kinds of low-cost, simple interventions that have made such a difference in the fight against other diseases in poor countries— think of polio vaccines and bed nets to prevent the spread of malaria, for example. In fact, similarly safe, effective, and inexpensive treatments exist for the most prevalent mental disorders.

Medications that relieve the most disabling symptoms of depression, psychosis, anxiety, and bipolar disorder have been available for five decades and now exist in relatively inexpensive generic formulations. A 2012 World Health Organization study showed that among 58 low- and middle-income countries, a typical course of such psychiatric medications costs, on average, approximately four percent of an individual's daily income. Although such treatments must be prescribed and managed by medical professionals, the paucity of psychiatrists in poorer countries would not necessarily present an obstacle to making psychiatric medications more widely available. After all, even in the developed world, most antidepressants and anti-anxiety medications are prescribed not by psychiatrists but by primary-care practitioners.

But perhaps the most promising new treatments for the most common mood and anxiety disorders have emerged thanks to technological innovation. As the Internet and mobile technology have spread, psychological treatments are no longer limited to those who can visit a psychotherapist's office. More than five billion people all over the world now have access to mobile devices that could allow them to receive psychotherapeutic interventions ranging from text messages that provide self-help strategies to computer games that incentivize positive changes in behavior. A group of psychiatric researchers in Australia recently found that a Web-based program reduced depressive and anxiety symptoms by allowing users to complete interactive modules on topics such as "managing fear and anxiety" and "tackling unhelpful thinking." And even in places where few people have smartphones, the spread of basic cellular service means that providers can still reach far more potential patients by phone than ever before.

OUT OF THE SHADOWS

Even if donors, international organizations, and governments came to better understand the massive costs associated with mental illness and the feasibility of treatments, genuine progress would still rely on a number of systemic changes. First, there is a basic need for increased awareness of the scope of the problem. In rich and poor countries alike, mental health advocates must do a better job of explaining to officials and the public the true costs of mental illness, encouraging people to understand how the problem affects not only individuals and families but also entire communities and economies. "No health without mental health" has become a rallying cry for reformers, but such slogans frequently fall on deaf ears. Mental health advocates could win more allies within the medical profession by drawing attention to the fact that improved mental health leads to better overall health.

Second, countries at every economic level must better integrate mental health care into their broader health-care systems. In wealthy countries, two simple steps would help: preparing more primary-care providers to treat mental disorders and creating incentives for mental health specialists and general medical practitioners to share facilities and establish partnerships, which would make it easier for people to get psychiatric and psychological care. In poorer countries, one step toward better integration would be to give community health workers, who already monitor basic health needs, the ability to screen for common mental disorders, as well. For example, nurses who help patients stick to their HIV medication regimens could incorporate mental health screening into their routines.

Finally, the international community needs to make a formal commitment to reducing the global economic burden of mental illness. Although mental illness affects the achievement of several of the UN's MDGs, such as empowering women, reducing child mortality, improving maternal health, and reversing the spread of HIV, the goals made no mention of mental health. Now, the process of drafting successors to the MDGs, the so-called Sustainable Development Goals, is well under way. Mental health advocates involved in the process are pushing for the establishment of specific targets, including a ten percent reduction in suicide by 2020 and a 20 percent increase in treatment for severe mental disorders by the same date. These are achievable goals, but meeting them will require political will, public and private investment, and coordination among the health, financial, social-service, and educational sectors.

Such steps will go a long way toward reducing the damage mental disorders inflict on societies and economies all over the world. But for such measures to succeed, policymakers and experts must first pull mental illness out of the shadows and into the center of debates about global public health.

The Calm Before the Storm

Why Volatility Signals Stability, and Vice Versa

Nassim Nicholas Taleb and Gregory F. Treverton

The aftermath of an airstrike in Aleppo, November 2014.

NASSIM NICHOLAS TALEB is Distinguished Professor of Risk Engineering at New York University's Polytechnic School of Engineering and the author of *Antifragile: Things That Gain From Disorder*.

GREGORY F. TREVERTON is Chair of the U.S. National Intelligence Council. From 2009 to 2014, he was Director of the RAND Corporation's Center for Global Risk and Security (where he wrote this article). This essay is adapted from a RAND risk-methodology report funded by the U.S. government.

E ven as protests spread across the Middle East in early 2011, the regime of Bashar al-Assad in Syria appeared immune from the upheaval. Assad had ruled comfortably for over a decade, having replaced his father, Hafez, who himself had held power for the previous three decades. Many pundits argued that Syria's sturdy police state, which exercised tight control over the country's people and economy, would survive the Arab Spring undisturbed. Compared with its neighbor Lebanon, Syria looked positively stable. Civil war had torn through Lebanon throughout much of the 1970s and 1980s, and the assassination of former Prime Minister Rafiq Hariri in 2005 had plunged the country into yet more chaos.

But appearances were deceiving: today, Syria is in a shambles, with the regime fighting for its very survival, whereas Lebanon has withstood the influx of Syrian refugees and the other considerable pressures of the civil war next door. Surprising as it may seem, the per capita death rate from violence in Lebanon in 2013 was lower than that in Washington, D.C. That same year, the body count of the Syrian conflict surpassed 100,000.

Why has seemingly stable Syria turned out to be the fragile regime, whereas always-in-turmoil Lebanon has so far proved robust? The answer is that prior to its civil war, Syria was exhibiting only pseudo-stability, its calm façade concealing deep structural vulnerabilities. Lebanon's chaos, paradoxically, signaled strength. Fifteen years of civil war had served to decentralize the state and bring about a more balanced sectarian power-sharing structure. Along with Lebanon's small size as an administrative unit, these factors added to its durability. So did the country's free-market economy. In Syria, the ruling Baath Party sought to control economic variability, replacing the lively chaos of the ancestral souk with the top-down, Soviet-style structure of the office building. This rigidity made Syria (and the other Baathist state, Iraq) much more vulnerable to disruption than Lebanon.

But Syria's biggest vulnerability was that it had no recent record of recovering from turmoil. Countries that have survived past bouts of chaos tend to be vaccinated against future ones. Thus, the best indicator of a country's future stability is not past stability but moderate volatility in the relatively recent past. As one of us, Nassim Nicholas Taleb, wrote in the 2007 book *The Black Swan*, "Dictatorships that do not appear volatile, like, say, Syria or Saudi Arabia, face a larger risk of chaos than, say, Italy, as the latter has been in a state of continual political turmoil since the second [world] war."

The divergent tales of Syria and Lebanon demonstrate that the best early warning signs of instability are found not in historical data but in underlying structural properties. Past experience can be extremely effective when it comes to detecting risks of cancer, crime, and earthquakes. But it is a bad bellwether of complex political and economic events, particularly so-called tail risks—events, such as coups and financial crises, that are highly unlikely but enormously consequential. For those, the evidence of risk comes too late to do anything about it, and a more sophisticated approach is required.

Thus, instead of trying in vain to predict such "Black Swan" events, it's much more fruitful to focus on how systems can handle disorder—in other words, to study how fragile they are. Although one cannot predict what events will befall a country, one can predict how events will affect a country. Some political systems can sustain an extraordinary amount of stress, while others fall apart at the onset of the slightest trouble. The good news is that it's possible to tell which are which by relying on the theory of fragility.

Simply put, fragility is aversion to disorder. Things that are fragile do not like variability, volatility, stress, chaos, and random events, which cause them to either gain little or suffer. A teacup, for example, will not benefit from any form of shock. It wants peace and predictability, something that is not possible in the long run, which is why time is an enemy to the fragile. What's more, things that are fragile respond to shock in a nonlinear fashion. With humans, for example, the harm from a ten-foot fall in no way equals ten times as much harm as from a one-foot fall. In political and economic terms, a $30 drop in the price of a barrel of oil is much more than twice as harmful to Saudi Arabia as a $15 drop.

For countries, fragility has five principal sources: a centralized governing system, an undiversified economy, excessive debt and leverage, a lack of political variability, and no history of surviving past shocks. Applying these criteria, the world map looks a lot different. Disorderly regimes come out as safer bets than commonly thought—and seemingly placid states turn out to be ticking time bombs.

THE CENTER CANNOT HOLD

The first marker of a fragile state is a concentrated decision-making system. On its face, centralization seems to make governments more efficient and thus more stable. But that stability is an illusion. Apart from in the military—the only sector that needs to be unified into a single structure—centralization contributes to fragility. Although centralization reduces deviations from the norm, making things appear to run more smoothly, it magnifies the consequences of those deviations that do occur. It concentrates turmoil in fewer but more severe episodes, which are disproportionately more harmful than cumulative small variations. In other words, centralization decreases local risks, such as provincial barons pocketing public funds, at the price of increasing systemic risks, such as disastrous national-level reforms. Accordingly, highly centralized states, such as the Soviet Union, are more fragile than decentralized ones, such as Switzerland, which is effectively composed of village-states.

States that centralize power often do so to suppress sectarian tension. That inability to handle diversity, whether political or ethnoreligious, further adds to their fragility. Although countries that allow their sectarian splits to remain out in the open may seem to experience political turmoil, they are considerably more stable than those that artificially repress those splits, which creates a discontented minority group that brews silently. Iraq, for example, had a Sunni-minority-led regime under Saddam Hussein that repressed the Shiites and the Kurds; the country overshot in the opposite direction after Prime Minister Nouri al-Maliki, a Shiite, took office in 2006 and began excluding the Sunnis. Indeed, research by the scholar Yaneer Bar-Yam has shown that states that have well-defined boundaries separating various ethnic groups experience less violence than those that attempt to integrate them. In other words, people are better next-door neighbors than roommates. Thus, in countries riven by sectarian divides, it makes more sense to give various groups their own fiefdoms than to force them to live under one roof, since the latter arrangement only serves to radicalize the repressed minority.

Moreover, centralization increases the odds of a military coup by making the levers of power easier to seize. Greece, for example, was highly centralized when a group of colonels overthrew the government in 1967. Italy might have appeared just as vulnerable around the same time, given that it also suffered from widespread social unrest and ideological conflict, but it was saved by its political decentralization and narrow geography. The various economic and political centers were both figuratively and literally far from one another, distance that prevented any single military faction from seizing power.

Just as states composed of semiautonomous units have fared well in the modern era, further back in history, the most resilient polities were city-states that operated under empires that provided a measure of protection, from Pax Romana to Pax Ottomana. But at the tail end of their existence, many empires began to centralize, including Pharaonic Egypt and the Ming dynasty in China. In both cases, the empires tightened the reins after, not before, they thrived, ruling out centralization as a cause of their success and fingering it as an explanation for their subsequent failure.

City-states both old and new—from Venice to Dubai to Geneva to Singapore—owe their success to their smallness. Those who compare political systems by looking at their character without taking into account their size are thus making an analytic error: city-states are remarkably diverse in terms of their political systems, from the most democratic (Venice) to the most enlightened but autocratic (Singapore). Just as an elephant is not a large mouse, China is not a bigger version of Singapore, even if the two share similar styles of government.

Again, consider Lebanon. For much of history, the Mediterranean was ringed by multilingual, religiously tolerant, and obsessively mercantile city-states, which accommodated a variety of empires. But most were eventually swallowed up by the modern nation-states. Alexandria was consumed by Egypt, Smyrna by Turkey, Thessaloniki by Greece, and Aleppo by Syria. Luckily for Lebanon, however, it was swallowed up by Beirut, not vice versa. After the collapse of the Ottoman Empire, the state of Lebanon was small and weak enough to get colonized by the city-state of Beirut. The result: over the past half century, living standards in Lebanon have risen in comparison to its peers. The country avoided the wave of statism that swept over the region with Gamal Abdel Nasser in Egypt and the Baath Party in Iraq and Syria, a trend that concentrated decision-making power and created dysfunctional bureaucracies, leading to many of the region's problems today.

UNSTEADY-STATE ECONOMY

The second soft spot is the absence of economic diversity. Economic concentration can be even more harmful than political centralization. Economists since David Ricardo have touted the gains in efficiency to be had if countries specialize in the sectors in which they hold a comparative advantage. But specialization makes a state more vulnerable in the face of random events.

For a state to be safe, the loss of a single source of income should not dramatically damage its overall economic condition. Places that depend on tourism, for example, are particularly susceptible to perceived instability (as Greece discovered after its economic crisis and Egypt discovered after its revolution), as well as unrelated events (as Hawaii found out immediately after 9/11) and even just the vagaries of fashion, as new hot spots replace older ones (as Tangier, Morocco, has come to recognize). Another common source of fragility is an economy built around a single commodity, such as Botswana, with its reliance on diamonds, or a single industry that accounts for the lion's share of exports, such as Japan's automobile sector. Even worse is when large state-sponsored or state-friendly enterprises dominate the economy; these tend to not only reduce competitiveness but also compound the downside risks of drops in demand for a particular commodity or product by responding only slowly and awkwardly to market signals.

The third source of fragility is also economic in nature: being highly indebted and highly leveraged. Debt is perhaps the single most critical source of fragility. It makes an entity more sensitive to shortfalls in revenue, and all the more so as those shortfalls accelerate. As Lehman Brothers experienced when it collapsed in 2008, as the confidence of investors wanes and requests for repayment grow, losses mount at an increasing rate. Debt issued by a state itself is perhaps the most vicious type of debt, because it doesn't turn into equity; instead, it becomes a permanent burden. Countries cannot easily go bankrupt—which, ironically, is the main reason people lend to them, believing that their investments are safe.

Leverage raises risks in much the same way. Dubai, for example, has plowed money into aggressive real estate projects, increasing its operating leverage and thus making any drops in revenue extremely threatening. Profit margins there are so thin that shortfalls could easily accelerate, which would rapidly push the emirate's companies into the red and drain state coffers. This means that Dubai, in spite of its admirable structure and governance, can rapidly go insolvent—as the world witnessed after the 2008 financial crisis, when Abu Dhabi had to bail it out.

THE VIRTUE OF VOLATILITY

The fourth source of fragility is a lack of political variability. Contrary to conventional wisdom, genuinely stable countries experience moderate political changes, continually switching governments and reversing their political orientations. By responding to pressures in the body politic, these changes promote stability, provided their magnitude is not too large—more like the gap between the Labour Party and the Conservative Party in the contemporary United Kingdom than that between the Jacobins and the royalists in revolutionary France. Moderate political variability also removes particular leaders from power, thus reducing cronyism in politics. When a state is decentralized, the variations are smoother still, since municipalities distribute decision-making power and allow for a plurality of political views.

It is political variability that makes democracies less fragile than autocracies. Italy is resilient precisely because it has been able to accommodate virtually constant political turmoil, training citizens for change and incubating institutions able to correct for mild instability. So far, perhaps predictably, none of the former dictatorships touched by the Arab Spring has demonstrated any such capacity. Egypt has reverted to military rule, and the others have fallen into varying degrees of chaos. Some states that emerged from autocratic rule without devolving into turmoil were able to develop means of accommodating change. Spain under Francisco Franco, for instance, over time became more and more an autocratic façade behind which the institutions of civil society could develop.

The fifth marker of fragility takes the proposition that there is no stability without volatility a step further: it is the lack of a record of surviving big shocks. States that have experienced a worst-case scenario in the recent past (say, around the previous two decades) and recovered from it are likely to be more stable than those that haven't. In part, this marker is simply providing information: countries that sustain chaos without falling apart reveal something about their strength that could not be discovered otherwise. But this marker also involves the idea of "antifragility," the property of gaining from disorder. Shocks to a state are educational, causing them to experience posttraumatic growth.

Look at Indonesia, Malaysia, the Philippines, South Korea, and Thailand. The fact that these countries weathered the 1997–98 Asian financial crisis suggests that they were robust enough to survive—and their impressive subsequent performance suggests that they might even have been antifragile, adjusting their institutions and practices based on the lessons of the crisis. Likewise, the fact that the former Soviet states have recovered from the collapse of the Soviet Union suggests that they are also relatively stable.

The idea is analogous to child rearing: parents want to protect their children from truly serious shocks that they might not survive but should not want to shelter them from the challenges in life that make them tougher.

THE BEAUTIFUL AND DAMNED

These five markers function best as warning signals. They cannot indicate with high confidence whether a given country is stable—no methodology can—but they certainly can reveal if a given country should cause worry. Those countries that score poorly on multiple criteria are particularly concerning, since these markers are compounding: qualifying as fragile on two counts is more than twice as dangerous as doing so on one. When it comes to overall fragility, countries can vary from exhibiting no signs of fragility to being very fragile.

Saudi Arabia is an easy call: it is extremely dependent on oil, has no political variability, and is highly centralized. Its oil wealth and powerful government have papered over the splits between its ethnoreligious units, with the Shiite minority living where the oil is. For the same reason, Bahrain should be considered extremely fragile, mainly on account of its repressed Shiite majority.

Egypt should also be considered fragile, given its only slight and cosmetic recovery from the chaos of the revolution and its highly centralized (and bureaucratic) government. So should Venezuela, which has a highly centralized political system, little political variability, an oil-based economy, and no record of surviving a massive shock. Some of the same problems apply to Russia. It remains highly dependent on oil and gas production and has a highly centralized political system. Its one redeeming factor is that it surmounted the difficult transition from the Soviet era. For that reason, it probably lies somewhere between moderately fragile and fragile.

Some countries are best categorized as fragile but possibly doing something about it. Greece holds enormous quantities of debt and has an inflexible political system, but it has begun to undertake an economic restructuring. (Time will tell whether this is the beginning of a new era of responsibility or a false start.) Iran has an effectively centralized government that exhibits little variability and an economy tied to oil and gas production, yet the regime has been tolerating (although only implicitly) a measure of political dissent. And although Iran is nominally a theocracy, unlike Saudi Arabia, it appears to have an extremely adaptive form of Islam that may accommodate modernization. Greece and Iran could transform into more robust states or lapse into fragility.

Moderately fragile states include Japan, given its highest-in-the-world debt-to-gdp ratio, long-term dominance by a single party, dependence on exports, and failure to fully recover from its "lost decade"; Brazil, which is growing increasingly centralized and bureaucratized; Nigeria, which is highly centralized and dependent on oil yet has rebounded from the economic and political turmoil of the 1980s and proved somewhat adaptable in the face of new threats, such as the Islamist insurgent group Boko Haram; and Turkey, which is highly centralized and has no track record of recovery. (In addition, Turkey's dependence on foreign investment is incompatible with its aggressive pro-Islamist foreign policy, which turns off Western investors.) India is perhaps best considered slightly fragile. Its political system is relatively decentralized and has adapted to rapid population growth and uneven economic progress, and its economy is somewhat reliant on exports.

Italy, paradoxically, shows no signs of fragility. It is effectively decentralized and has bounced back from perennial political crises. It also experiences a great deal of harmless political variability, cycling through 14 prime ministerial terms in the past 25 years. France, by contrast, is more fragile—centralized (in spite of the lip service it pays to decentralization), indebted, and without a demonstrated comeback. The country is at risk of economic trauma, which would raise the danger of erratic political reactions. Those, in turn, would likely enhance the appeal of right-wing factions and radicalize the country's significant Muslim minority.

Then there is the China puzzle. China's stunning economic growth makes its future hard to assess. The country has recuperated remarkably well from the major shocks of the Maoist period. That era, however, ended nearly four decades ago, and so the recovery is hardly a recent comeback and thus less certain to protect against future shocks. What's more, China's political system is highly centralized, its economy is dependent on exports to the West, and its government has been on a borrowing binge as of late, making the country more vulnerable to slowdowns in both domestic and foreign growth. Are the gains from past turmoil big enough to offset the weakness from debt and centralization? The most likely answer is no—that what gains China has accrued by learning from trauma are dwarfed by its burdens. With each passing year, those lessons recede further into the past, and the prospects of a Black Swan of Beijing loom larger. But the sooner that event happens, the better China will emerge in the long run.

The Failure of Multiculturalism

Community Versus Society in Europe

Kenan Malik

Boxed in: public housing for asylum seekers in Berlin, January 2015.

Thirty years ago, many Europeans saw multiculturalism— the embrace of an inclusive, diverse society—as an answer to Europe's social problems. Today, a growing number consider it to be a cause of them. That perception has led some mainstream politicians, including British Prime Minister David Cameron

KENAN MALIK is a monthly columnist for The International New York Times and the author, most recently, of *The Quest for a Moral Compass: A Global History of Ethics*. Follow him on Twitter @kenanmalik.

and German Chancellor Angela Merkel, to publicly denounce multiculturalism and speak out against its dangers. It has fueled the success of far-right parties and populist politicians across Europe, from the Party for Freedom in the Netherlands to the National Front in France. And in the most extreme cases, it has inspired obscene acts of violence, such as Anders Behring Breivik's homicidal rampage on the Norwegian island of Utoya in July 2011.

How did this transformation come about? According to multiculturalism's critics, Europe has allowed excessive immigration without demanding enough integration—a mismatch that has eroded social cohesion, undermined national identities, and degraded public trust. Multiculturalism's proponents, on the other hand, counter that the problem is not too much diversity but too much racism.

But the truth about multiculturalism is far more complex than either side will allow, and the debate about it has often devolved into sophistry. Multiculturalism has become a proxy for other social and political issues: immigration, identity, political disenchantment, working-class decline. Different countries, moreover, have followed distinct paths. The United Kingdom has sought to give various ethnic communities an equal stake in the political system. Germany has encouraged immigrants to pursue separate lives in lieu of granting them citizenship. And France has rejected multicultural policies in favor of assimilationist ones. The specific outcomes have also varied: in the United Kingdom, there has been communal violence; in Germany, Turkish communities have drifted further from mainstream society; and in France, the relationship between the authorities and North African communities has become highly charged. But everywhere, the overarching consequences have been the same: fragmented societies, alienated minorities, and resentful citizenries.

As a political tool, multiculturalism has functioned as not merely a response to diversity but also a means of constraining it. And that insight reveals a paradox. Multicultural policies accept as a given that societies are diverse, yet they implicitly assume that such diversity ends at the edges of minority communities. They seek to institutionalize diversity by putting people into ethnic and cultural boxes—into a singular, homogeneous Muslim community, for example—and defining their needs and rights accordingly. Such policies, in other words, have helped create the very divisions they were meant to manage.

THE DIVERSITY MYTH

Untangling the many strands of the multiculturalism debate requires understanding the concept itself. The term "multicultural" has come to define both a society that is particularly diverse, usually as a result of immigration, and the policies necessary to manage such a society. It thus embodies both a description of society and a prescription for dealing with it. Conflating the two—perceived problem with supposed solution—has tightened the knot at the heart of the debate. Unpicking that knot requires a careful evaluation of each.

Both proponents and critics of multiculturalism broadly accept the premise that mass immigration has transformed European societies by making them more diverse. To a certain extent, this seems self-evidently true. Today, Germany is the world's second most popular immigrant destination, after the United States. In 2013, more than ten million people, or just over 12 percent of the population, were born abroad. In Austria, that figure was 16 percent; in Sweden, 15 percent; and in France and the United Kingdom, around 12 percent. From a historical perspective, however, the claim that these countries are more plural than ever is not as straightforward as it may seem. Nineteenth-century European societies may look homogeneous from the vantage point of today, but that is not how those societies saw themselves then.

Consider France. In the years of the French Revolution, for instance, only half the population spoke French and only around 12 percent spoke it correctly. As the historian Eugen Weber showed, modernizing and unifying France in the revolution's aftermath required a traumatic and lengthy process of cultural, educational, political, and economic self-colonization. That effort created the modern French state and gave birth to notions of French (and European) superiority over non-European cultures. But it also reinforced a sense of how socially and culturally disparate most of the population still was. In an address to the Medico-Psychological Society of Paris in 1857, the Christian socialist Philippe Buchez wondered how it could happen that "within a population such as ours, races may form—not merely one, but several races—so miserable, inferior and bastardised that they may be classed as below the most inferior savage races, for their inferiority is sometimes beyond cure." The "races" that caused Buchez such anxiety were not immigrants from Africa or Asia but the rural poor in France.

In the Victorian era, many Britons, too, viewed the urban working class and the rural poor as the other. A vignette of working-class life in East London's Bethnal Green, appearing in an 1864 edition of *The Saturday Review*, a well-read liberal magazine of the era, was typical of Victorian middle-class attitudes. "The Bethnal Green poor," the story explained, were "a caste apart, a race of whom we know nothing, whose lives are of quite different complexion from ours, persons with whom we have no point of contact." Much the same was true, the article suggested, of "the great mass of the agricultural poor." Although the distinctions between slaves and masters were considered more "glaring" than those separating the moneyed and the poor, they offered "a very fair parallel"; indeed, the differences were so profound that they prevented "anything like association or companionship."

Today, Bethnal Green represents the heart of the Bangladeshi community in East London. Many white Britons see its inhabitants as the new Bethnal Green poor, culturally and racially distinct from themselves. Yet only those on the political fringes would compare the differences between white Britons and their Bangladeshi neighbors with those of masters and slaves. The social and cultural differences between a Victorian gentleman or factory owner, on the one hand, and a farm hand or a machinist, on the other, were in reality much greater than those between a white resident and a resident of Bangladeshi origin are today. However much they may view each other as different, a 16-year-old of Bangladeshi origin living in Bethnal Green and a white 16-year-old probably wear the same clothes, listen to the same music, and follow the same soccer club. The shopping mall, the sports field, and the Internet bind them together, creating a set of experiences and cultural practices more common than any others in the past.

A similar historical amnesia plagues discussions surrounding immigration. Many critics of multiculturalism suggest that immigration to Europe today is unlike that seen in previous times. In his book *Reflections on the Revolution in Europe*, the journalist Christopher Caldwell suggests that prior to World War II, immigrants to European countries came almost exclusively from the continent and therefore assimilated easily. "Using the word *immigration* to describe intra-European movements," Caldwell argues, "makes only slightly more sense than describing a New Yorker as an 'immigrant' to California." According to Caldwell, prewar immigration between European nations differed from postwar immigration from outside Europe because "immigration from neighboring countries does not provoke the most worrisome immigration questions, such as 'How well will they fit in?' 'Is assimilation what they want?' and, most of all, 'Where are their true loyalties?'"

Yet these very questions greeted European immigrants in the prewar years. As the scholar Max Silverman has written, the notion that France assimilated immigrants from elsewhere in Europe with ease before World War II is a "retrospective illusion." And much the same is true of the United Kingdom. In 1903, witnesses to the Royal Commission on Alien Immigration expressed fears that newcomers to the United Kingdom would be inclined to live "according to their traditions, usages and customs." There were also concerns, as the newspaper editor J. L. Silver put it, that "the debilitated sickly and vicious products of Europe" could be "grafted onto the English stock." The country's first immigration law, the 1905 Aliens Act, was designed principally to stem the flow of European Jews. Without such a law, then Prime Minister Arthur Balfour argued at the time, British "nationality would not be the same and would not be the nationality we should desire to be our heirs through the ages yet to come." The echoes of contemporary anxieties are unmistakable.

RACE TO THE TOP

Whether contemporary Europe really is more plural than it was in the nineteenth century remains subject to debate, but the fact that Europeans perceive it to be more diverse is unquestionable. This owes in large part to changes in how people define social differences. A century and a half ago, class was a far more important frame for understanding social interactions. However difficult it is to conceive of now, many at the time saw racial distinctions in terms of differences not in skin color but in class or social standing. Most nineteenth-century thinkers were concerned not with the strangers who crossed their countries' borders but with those who inhabited the dark spaces within them.

Over the past few decades, however, class has diminished in importance in Europe, both as a political category and as a marker of social identity. At the same time, culture has become an increasingly central medium through which people perceive social differences. The shift reflects broader trends. The ideological divides that characterized politics for much of the past 200 years have receded, and the old distinctions between left and right have become less meaningful. As the working classes have lost economic and political power, labor organizations and collectivistic ideologies have declined. The market, meanwhile, has expanded into almost every nook and cranny of social life. And institutions that traditionally brought disparate individuals together, from trade unions to the church, have faded from public life.

As a result, Europeans have begun to see themselves and their social affiliations in a different way. Increasingly, they define social solidarity not in political terms but rather in terms of ethnicity, culture, or faith. And they are concerned less with determining the kind of society they want to create than with defining the community to which they belong. These two matters are, of course, intimately related, and any sense of social identity must take both into account.

But as the ideological spectrum has narrowed and as the mechanisms for change have eroded, the politics of ideology have given way to the politics of identity. It is against this background that Europeans have come to view their homelands as particularly, even impossibly, diverse—and have formulated ways of responding.

UNDER MY UMBRELLA

In describing contemporary European societies as exceptionally diverse, multiculturalism is clearly flawed. What, then, of multiculturalism's prescription for managing that supposed diversity? Over the past three decades, many European nations have adopted multicultural policies, but they have done so in distinct ways. Comparing just two of these histories, that of the United Kingdom and that of Germany, and understanding what they have in common, reveals much about multiculturalism itself.

One of the most prevalent myths in European politics is that governments adopted multicultural policies because minorities wanted to assert their differences. Although questions about cultural assimilation have certainly engrossed political elites, they have not, until relatively recently, preoccupied immigrants themselves. When large numbers of immigrants from the Caribbean, India, and Pakistan arrived in the United Kingdom during the late 1940s and 1950s to fill labor shortages, British officials feared that they might undermine the country's sense of identity. As a government report warned in 1953, "A large coloured community as a noticeable feature of our social life would weaken . . . the concept of England or Britain to which people of British stock throughout the Commonwealth are attached."

The immigrants brought with them traditions and mores from their homelands, of which they were often very proud. But they were rarely preoccupied with preserving their cultural differences, nor did they generally consider culture to be a political issue. What troubled them was not a desire to be treated differently but the fact that they were treated differently. Racism and inequality, not religion and ethnicity, constituted their key concerns. In the following decades, a new generation of black and Asian activists, forming groups such as the Asian Youth Movements and the Race Today Collective, acted on those grievances, organizing strikes and protests challenging workplace discrimination, deportations, and police brutality. These efforts came to explosive climax in a series of riots that tore through the United Kingdom's inner cities in the late 1970s and early 1980s.

At that point, British authorities recognized that unless minority communities were given a political stake in the system, tensions would continue to threaten urban stability. It was in this context that multicultural policies emerged. The state, at both the national and the local level, pioneered a new strategy of drawing black and Asian communities into the mainstream political process by designating specific organizations or community leaders to represent their interests. At its heart, the approach redefined the concepts of racism and equality. Racism now meant not simply the denial of equal rights but also the denial of the right to be different. And equality no longer entailed possessing rights that transcended race, ethnicity, culture, and faith; it meant asserting different rights because of them.

Consider the case of Birmingham, the United Kingdom's second most populous city. In 1985, the city's Handsworth area was engulfed by riots sparked by a simmering resentment of poverty, joblessness, and, in particular, police harassment. Two people died and dozens were injured in the violence. In the aftermath of the unrest, the city council attempted to engage minorities by creating nine so-called umbrella groups—organizations that were supposed to advocate for their members on matters of city policy. These committees decided on the needs of each community, how and to whom resources should be disbursed, and how political power should be distributed. They effectively became surrogate voices for ethnically defined fiefdoms.

The city council had hoped to draw minorities into the democratic process, but the groups struggled to define their individual and collective mandates. Some of them, such as the African and

Caribbean People's Movement, represented an ethnic group, whereas others, such as the Council of Black-Led Churches, were also religious. Diversity among the groups was matched by diversity within them; not all the people supposedly represented by the Bangladeshi Islamic Projects Consultative Committee, for example, were equally devout. Yet the city council's plan effectively assigned every member of a minority to a discrete community, defined each group's needs as a whole, and set the various organizations in competition with one another for city resources. And anyone who fell outside these defined communities was effectively excluded from the multicultural process altogether.

The problem with Birmingham's policies, observed Joy Warmington, director of what was then the Birmingham Race Action Partnership (now BRAP), a charitable organization working to reduce inequality, in 2005, is that they "have tended to emphasize ethnicity as a key to entitlement. It's become accepted as good practice to allocate resources on ethnic or faith lines. So rather than thinking of meeting people's needs or about distributing resources equitably, organizations are forced to think about the distribution of ethnicity." The consequences were catastrophic. In October 2005, two decades after the original Handsworth riots, violence broke out in the neighboring area of Lozells. In 1985, Asian, black, and white demonstrators had taken to the streets together to protest poverty, unemployment, and police harassment. In 2005, the fighting was between blacks and Asians. The spark had been a rumor, never substantiated, that a group of Asian men had raped a Jamaican girl. The fighting lasted a full weekend.

Why did two communities that had fought side by side in 1985 fight against each other in 2005? The answer lies largely in Birmingham's multicultural policies. As one academic study of Birmingham's policies observed, "The model of engagement through Umbrella Groups tended to result in competition between BME [black and minority ethnic] communities for resources. Rather than prioritizing needs and cross-community working, the different Umbrella Groups generally attempted to maximize their own interests."

The council's policies, in other words, not only bound people more closely to particular identities but also led them to fear and resent other groups as competitors for power and influence. An individual's identity had to be affirmed as distinctive from the identities of those from other groups: being Bangladeshi in Birmingham also meant being not Irish, not Sikh, and not African Caribbean. The consequence was the creation of what the economist Amartya Sen has termed "plural monoculturalism"—a policy driven by the myth that society is made up of distinct, uniform cultures that dance around one another. The result in Birmingham was to entrench divisions between black and Asian communities to such an extent that those divisions broke out into communal violence.

SEPARATE AND UNEQUAL

Germany's road to multiculturalism was different from the United Kingdom's, although the starting point was the same. Like many countries in western Europe, Germany faced an immense labor shortage in the years following World War II and actively recruited foreign workers. Unlike in the United Kingdom, the new workers came not from former colonies but from the countries around the Mediterranean: first from Greece, Italy, and Spain, and then from Turkey. They also came not as immigrants, still less as potential citizens, but as so-called Gastarbeiter (guest workers), who were expected to return to their countries of origin when the German economy no longer required their services.

Over time, however, these guests, the vast majority of them Turks, went from being a temporary necessity to a permanent presence. This was partly because Germany continued to rely on their labor and partly because the immigrants, and more so their children, came to see Germany as their home. But the German state continued to treat them as outsiders and refuse them citizenship.

German citizenship was, until recently, based on the principle of *jus sanguinis*, by which one can acquire citizenship only if one's parents were citizens. The principle excluded from citizenship not just first-generation immigrants but also their German-born children.

In 1999, a new nationality law made it easier for immigrants to acquire citizenship. Yet most Turks remain outsiders. Out of the three million people of Turkish origin in Germany today, only some 800,000 have managed to acquire citizenship.

Instead of welcoming immigrants as equals, German politicians dealt with the so-called Turkish problem through a policy of multiculturalism. Beginning in the 1980s, the government encouraged Turkish immigrants to preserve their own culture, language, and lifestyle. The policy did not represent a respect for diversity so much as a convenient means of avoiding the issue of how to create a common, inclusive culture. And its main consequence was the emergence of parallel communities.

First-generation immigrants were broadly secular, and those who were religious were rarely hard-line in their beliefs and practices. Today, almost one-third of adult Turks in Germany regularly attend mosque, a higher rate than among other Turkish communities in western Europe and even in many parts of Turkey. Similarly, first-generation Turkish women almost never wore headscarves; now many of their daughters do. Without any incentive to participate in the national community, many Turks don't bother learning German.

At the same time that Germany's multicultural policies have encouraged Turks to approach German society with indifference, they have led Germans to view Turkish culture with increasing antagonism. Popular notions of what it means to be German have come to be defined partly in opposition to the perceived values and beliefs of the excluded immigrant community. A 2011 survey conducted by the French polling firm Ifop showed that 40 percent of Germans considered the presence of Islamic communities "a threat" to their national identity. Another poll, conducted by Germany's Bielefeld University in 2005, suggested that three out of four Germans believed that Muslim culture did not fit into the Western world. Anti-Muslim groups, such as Patriotic Europeans Against the Islamization of the West, or PEGIDA, are on the rise, and anti-immigration protests held in cities across the country this past January were some of the largest in recent memory. Many German politicians, including Merkel, have taken a strong stance against the anti-Muslim movement. But the damage has already been done.

SUBCONTRACTING POLICY

In both the United Kingdom and Germany, governments failed to recognize the complexity, elasticity, and sheer contrariness of identity. Personal identities emerge out of relationships—not merely personal ties but social ones, too—and constantly mutate.

Take Muslim identity. Today there is much talk in European countries of a so-called Muslim community—of its views, its needs, its aspirations. But the concept is entirely new. Until the late 1980s, few Muslim immigrants to Europe thought of themselves as belonging to any such thing. That wasn't because they were few in number. In France, Germany, and the United Kingdom, for example, there were already large and well-established South Asian, North African, and Turkish immigrant communities by the 1980s.

The first generation of North African immigrants to France was broadly secular, as was the first generation of Turkish immigrants to Germany. By contrast, the first wave of South Asian immigrants to arrive in the United Kingdom after World War II was more religious. Yet even they thought of themselves not as Muslims first but as Punjabis or Bengalis or Sylhetis. Although pious, they wore their faith lightly. Many men drank alcohol. Few women wore a hijab, let alone a burqa or a niqab (a full-faced veil). Most attended mosque only occasionally. Islam was not, in their eyes, an all-encompassing philosophy. Their faith defined their relationship with God, not a sacrosanct public identity.

Members of the second generation of Britons with Muslim backgrounds were even less likely to identify with their religion. The same went for those whose parents were Hindu or Sikh. Religious organizations were barely visible within minority communities. The organizations that bound immigrants together were primarily secular and often political; in the United Kingdom, for example, such groups included the Asian Youth Movements, which fought racism, and the Indian Workers' Association, which focused on labor rights.

Only in the late 1980s did the question of cultural differences become important. A generation that, ironically, is far more integrated and westernized than the first turned out to be the more insistent on maintaining its alleged distinctiveness. The reasons for this shift are complex. Partly they lie in a tangled web of larger social, political, and economic changes over the past half century, such as the collapse of the left and the rise of identity politics. Partly they lie in international developments, such as the Iranian Revolution of 1979 and the Bosnian war of the early 1990s, both of which played an important role in fostering a more heightened sense of Muslim identity in Europe. And partly they lie in European multicultural policies.

Group identities are not natural categories; they arise out of social interaction. But as cultural categories received official sanction, certain identities came to seem fixed. In channeling financial resources and political power through ethnically based organizations, governments provided a form of authenticity to certain ethnic identities and denied it to others.

Multicultural policies seek to build a bridge between the state and minority communities by looking to particular community organizations and leaders to act as intermediaries. Rather than appeal to Muslims and other minorities as citizens, politicians tend to assume minorities' true loyalty is to their faith or ethnic community. In effect, governments subcontract their political responsibilities out to minority leaders.

Such leaders are, however, rarely representative of their communities. That shouldn't be a surprise: no single group or set of leaders could represent a single white community. Some white Europeans are conservative, many are liberal, and still others are communist or neofascist. And most whites would not see their interests as specifically "white." A white Christian probably has more in common with a black Christian than with a white atheist; a white socialist would likely think more like a Bangladeshi socialist than like a white conservative; and so on. Muslims and Sikhs and African Caribbeans are no different; herein rests the fundamental flaw of multiculturalism.

ASSIMILATE NOW

France's policy of assimilationism is generally regarded as the polar opposite of multiculturalism, which French politicians have proudly rejected. Unlike the rest of Europe, they insist, France treats every individual as a citizen rather than as a member of a particular racial, ethnic, or cultural group. In reality, however, France is as socially divided as Germany or the United Kingdom, and in a strikingly similar way.

Questions surrounding French social policy, and the country's social divisions, came sharply into focus in Paris this past January, when Islamist gunmen shot 12 people dead at the offices of the satirical magazine *Charlie Hebdo* and four Jews in a kosher supermarket. French politicians had long held multicultural policies responsible for nurturing homegrown jihadists in the United Kingdom. Now they had to answer for why such terrorists had been nurtured in assimilationist France, too.

It is often claimed that there are some five million Muslims in France—supposedly the largest Muslim community in western Europe. In fact, those of North African origin in France, who have been lumped into this group, have never constituted a single community, still less a religious one. Immigrants from North Africa have been broadly secular and indeed often hostile to religion. A 2006 report by the Pew Research Center showed that 42 percent of Muslims in France identified themselves as French citizens first—more than in Germany, Spain, or the United Kingdom. A growing number have, in recent years, become attracted to Islam. But even today, according to a 2011 study by Ifop, only 40 percent identify themselves as observant Muslims, and only 25 percent attend Friday prayers.

Those of North African origin in France are also often described as immigrants. In fact, the majority are second-generation French citizens, born in France and as French as any voter for the National Front. The use of the terms "Muslim" and "immigrant" as labels for French citizens of North African origin is not, however, accidental. It is part of the process whereby the state casts such citizens as the other—as not really part of the French nation.

As in the United Kingdom, in France, the first generation of post–World War II immigrants faced considerable racism, and the second generation was far less willing to accept social discrimination, unemployment, and police brutality. They organized, largely through secular organizations, and took to the streets, often in violent protest. The riots that swept through French cities in the fall of 2005 exposed the fractures in French society as clearly as had those that engulfed British cities two decades earlier.

During the 1970s and early 1980s, the French authorities took a relatively laid-back stance on multiculturalism, generally tolerating cultural and religious differences at a time when few within minority communities expressed their identities in cultural or religious terms. French President François Mitterrand even coined the slogan *le droit à la différence* (the right to difference). As tensions within North African communities became more open and as the National Front emerged as a political force, Paris abandoned that approach for a more hard-line position. The riots in 2005, and the disaffection they expressed, were presented less as a response to racism than as an expression of Islam's growing threat to France. In principle, the French authorities rejected the multicultural approach of the United Kingdom. In practice, however, they treated North African immigrants and their descendents in a "multicultural" way—as a single community, primarily a Muslim one. Concerns about Islam came to reflect larger anxieties about the crisis of values and identity that now beset France.

A much-discussed 2013 poll conducted by the French research group Ipsos and the Centre de Recherches Politiques, or CEVIPOF, at the Institut d'Études Politiques de Paris (known as Sciences Po) found that 50 percent of the French population believed that the economic and cultural "decline" of their country was "inevitable."

Fewer than one-third thought that French democracy worked well, and 62 percent considered "most" politicians to be "corrupt." The pollsters' report described a fractured France, divided along tribal lines, alienated from mainstream politics, distrustful of national leaders, and resentful of Muslims. The main sentiment driving French society, the report concluded, was "fear."

In the United Kingdom, multicultural policies were at once an acknowledgment of a more fractured society and the source of one. In France, assimilationist policies have, paradoxically, had the same result. Faced with a distrustful and disengaged public, politicians have attempted to reassert a common French identity. But unable to define clearly the ideas and values that characterize the country, they have done so primarily by sowing hostility toward symbols of alienness—by banning the burqa, for example, in 2010.

Instead of accepting North Africans as full citizens, French policy has tended to ignore the racism and discrimination they have faced. Many in France view its citizens of North African origin not as French but as Arab or Muslim. But second-generation North Africans are often as estranged from their parents' culture and mores—and from mainstream Islam—as they are from wider French society. They are caught not between two cultures, as it is often claimed, but without one. As a consequence, some of them have turned to Islamism, and a few have expressed their inchoate rage through jihadist violence.

At the same time, French assimilationist policies have exacerbated the sense of disengagement felt by traditional working-class communities. The social geographer Christophe Guilluy has coined the phrase "the peripheral France" to describe those people "pushed out by the deindustrialization and gentrification of the urban centers," who "live away from the economic and decision-making centers, in a state of social non-integration," and have thus come to "feel excluded." The peripheral France has emerged mainly as a result of economic and political developments. But like many parts of the country's North African communities, it has come to see its marginalization through the lens of cultural and ethnic identity.

According to the 2013 Ipsos-CEVIPOF poll, seven out of ten people thought there were "too many foreigners in France," and 74 percent considered Islam to be incompatible with French society. Presenting Islam as a threat to French values has not only strengthened culture's political role but also sharpened popular disenchantment with mainstream politics.

In the past, disaffection, whether within North African or white working-class communities, would have led to direct political action. Today, however, both groups are expressing their grievances through identity politics. In their own ways, racist populism and radical Islamism are each expressions of a similar kind of social disengagement in an era of identity politics.

ANOTHER WAY

Multiculturalism and assimilationism are different policy responses to the same problem: the fracturing of society. And yet both have had the effect of making things worse. It's time, then, to move beyond the increasingly sterile debate between the two approaches. And that requires making three kinds of distinctions.

First, Europe should separate diversity as a lived experience from multiculturalism as a political process. The experience of living in a society made diverse by mass immigration should be welcomed. Attempts to institutionalize such diversity through the formal recognition of cultural differences should be resisted.

Second, Europe should distinguish colorblindness from blindness to racism. The assimilationist resolve to treat everyone equally as citizens, rather than as bearers of specific racial or cultural histories, is valuable. But that does not mean that the state should ignore discrimination against particular groups. Citizenship has no meaning if different classes of citizens are treated differently, whether because of multicultural policies or because of racism.

Finally, Europe should differentiate between peoples and values. Multiculturalists argue that societal diversity erodes the possibility of common values. Similarly, assimilationists suggest that such values are possible only within a more culturally—and, for some, ethnically—homogeneous society. Both regard minority communities as homogeneous wholes, attached to a particular set of cultural traits, faiths, beliefs, and values, rather than as constituent parts of a modern democracy.

The real debate should be not between multiculturalism and assimilationism but between two forms of the former and two forms of the latter. An ideal policy would marry multiculturalism's embrace of actual diversity, rather than its tendency to institutionalize differences, and assimilationism's resolve to treat everyone as citizens, rather than its tendency to construct a national identity by characterizing certain groups as alien to the nation. In practice, European countries have done the opposite. They have enacted either multicultural policies that place communities in constricting boxes or assimilationist ones that distance minorities from the mainstream.

Moving forward, Europe must rediscover a progressive sense of universal values, something that the continent's liberals have largely abandoned, albeit in different ways. On the one hand, there is a section of the left that has combined relativism and multiculturalism, arguing that the very notion of universal values is in some sense racist. On the other, there are those, exemplified by such French assimilationists as the philosopher Bernard-Henri Lévy, who insist on upholding traditional Enlightenment values but who do so in a tribal fashion that presumes a clash of civilizations.

There has also been a guiding assumption throughout Europe that immigration and integration must be managed through state policies and institutions. Yet real integration, whether of immigrants or of indigenous groups, is rarely brought about by the actions of the state; it is shaped primarily by civil society, by the individual bonds that people form with one another, and by the organizations they establish to further their shared political and social interests. It is the erosion of such bonds and institutions that has proved so problematic—that links assimilationist policy failures to multicultural ones and that explains why social disengagement is a feature not simply of immigrant communities but of the wider society, too. To repair the damage that disengagement has done, and to revive a progressive universalism, Europe needs not so much new state policies as a renewal of civil society.

The Resistible Rise of Vladimir Putin

Russia's Nightmare Dressed Like a Daydream

Stephen Kotkin

MAXIM ZMEYEV / COURTESY REUTERS

How did twenty-first-century Russia end up, yet again, in personal rule? An advanced industrial country of 142 million people, it has no enduring political parties that organize and respond to voter preferences. The military is sprawling yet tame; the immense secret police are effectively in one man's pocket.

STEPHEN KOTKIN is Professor of History and International Affairs at Princeton University and the author of *Stalin, vol. 1, Paradoxes of Power, 1878–1928*.

The hydrocarbon sector is a personal bank, and indeed much of the economy is increasingly treated as an individual fiefdom. Mass media move more or less in lockstep with the commands of the presidential administration. Competing interest groups abound, but there is no rival center of power. In late October 2014, after a top aide to Russia's president told the annual forum of the Valdai Discussion Club, which brings together Russian and foreign experts, that Russians understand "if there is no Putin, there is no Russia," the pundit Stanislav Belkovsky observed that "the search for Russia's national idea, which began after the dissolution of the Soviet Union, is finally over. Now, it is evident that Russia's national idea is Vladimir Vladimirovich Putin."

Russia is classified as a high-income economy by the World Bank (having a per capita GDP exceeding $14,000). Its unemployment remains low (around five percent); until recently, consumer spending had been expanding at more than five percent annually; life expectancy has been rising; and Internet penetration exceeds that of some countries in the European Union. But Russia is now beset by economic stagnation alongside high inflation, its labor productivity remains dismally low, and its once-vaunted school system has deteriorated alarmingly. And it is astonishingly corrupt. Not only the bullying central authorities in Moscow but regional state bodies, too, have been systematically criminalizing revenue streams, while giant swaths of territory lack basic public services and local vigilante groups proliferate. Across the country, officials who have purchased their positions for hefty sums team up with organized crime syndicates and use friendly prosecutors and judges to extort and expropriate rivals. President Vladimir Putin's vaunted "stability," in short, has turned into spoliation. But Putin has been in power for 15 years, and there is no end in sight. Stalin ruled for some three decades; Brezhnev for almost two. Putin, still relatively young and healthy, looks set to top the latter and might even outdo the former.

In some ways, observers are still trying to fathom how the revolt against tsarist autocracy in 1917—the widest mass revolution in history up to that point—culminated in a regime unaccountable to itself, let alone to the masses. Now, after the mass mobilizations for democracy that accompanied and followed the 1991 Soviet collapse, a new authoritarianism has taken shape. Of course, Putin's dictatorship differs substantially from the Soviet communist version. Today's Russia has no single ideology and no disciplined ruling party, and although it lacks the rule of law, it does allow private property and free movement across borders. Still, the country is back in a familiar place, a one-man regime.

The methods Putin used to fix the corrupt, dysfunctional post-Soviet state have produced yet another corrupt, dysfunctional state. Putin himself complains publicly that only about 20 percent of his decisions get implemented, with the rest being ignored or circumvented unless he intervenes forcefully with the interest groups and functionaries concerned. But he cannot intervene directly with every boss, governor, and official in the country on every issue. Many underlings invoke Putin's name and do what they want. Personal systems of rule convey immense power on the ruler in select strategic areas—the secret police, control of cash flow—but they are ultimately ineffective and self-defeating.

Russia just might be able to get out of this trap, in part because of the severity of the various crises currently besetting Putin's regime. But perversely, even that hopeful scenario would require yet another act of personal rule.

FROM LENINGRAD TO MOSCOW

Putin was born in Soviet Leningrad in 1952, the only surviving child of parents who had lived through the Nazi siege of the city a decade earlier. He grew up in a rough section of Peter the Great's showcase, took up martial arts, graduated with a degree in law from Leningrad State University, and begged his way into the KGB, eventually being posted to Dresden, East Germany, in 1985.

In 1990, after the fall of the Berlin Wall, the KGB recalled him to Leningrad and assigned him to his alma mater, where his former law professor Anatoly Sobchak still taught part time. Sobchak eventually became chair of the city council and then mayor, and Putin served as his top deputy, responsible for difficult assignments, including feeding the city's large population during the years of post-Soviet economic depression. He discovered that Leningrad's self-styled democrats could get almost nothing done and that he could embezzle money both to help address the city's challenges and to enrich himself and his cronies. When Sobchak lost a bid for reelection in 1996, Putin found himself unemployed at 43. But a year later, through connections (notably Alexei Kudrin, another official in the Sobchak mayoralty who had become deputy chief of staff to Russian President Boris Yeltsin), Putin moved to Moscow and obtained a series of positions in the presidential administration, the successor to the old Soviet central-party apparatus.

There are indications that Putin might have coveted the lucrative, powerful CEO job at Gazprom, Russia's monopoly gas behemoth, but if so, it eluded him. Then, in July 1998, lightning struck: Yeltsin appointed the former lieutenant colonel above hundreds of higher-ranking secret police officers to head the FSB, the successor to the KGB—and the following year appointed him first acting prime minister of the Russian Federation and then acting president. So the simplest answer to the question of how Putin came to power is that he was selected.

Yeltsin's inner circle, known as "the Family"—in particular, Valentin Yumashev (the ghostwriter of Yeltsin's autobiographies) and Yumashev's future wife, Yeltsin's daughter Tatyana—picked Putin over others who failed their auditions. He had shown a basic competence in administration and had demonstrated loyalty (having arranged in 1997 for Sobchak, then under threat of arrest, to escape to France without submitting to Russian passport control). It was hoped that he would protect the Family's interests, and maybe those of Russia as well. Putin secured victory in the March 2000 presidential election through control of the country's main television station, Channel One (thanks to Boris Berezovsky, a secondary member of the Family); ruthless manipulation of the Chechen terrorist threat; and access to all the perks of incumbency. Some fraud, too, cannot be excluded. In the reported results, Putin received nearly 40 million votes, 53 percent of those cast, a majority that enabled him to avoid a runoff. Second place (29 percent) went to the Communist Party candidate-bogeyman. Nine other candidates split the rest of the votes.

Interestingly, when Putin took office, he had little effective power. His chief of staff, Alexander Voloshin, was a core member of the Family and would remain in his commanding position for two more years. Berezovsky continued to control Channel One, and the second most important station, privately owned NTV, belonged to the independent actor Vladimir Gusinsky. The mammoth cash flow generated by the state gas monopoly had been largely privatized into the hands of a cabal led by Rem Vyakhirev (a protégé of the former Soviet gas minister, later the Russian prime minister, Viktor Chernomyrdin), and much of the oil industry had been formally privatized, a lot of it into a huge new company, Yukos, controlled by Mikhail Khodorkovsky. Russia's then 89 regions were in the hands of governors who answered to no one. Chechnya had de facto independence. The Russian state was floundering.

Bit by bit, however, using stealth and dirty tricks, Putin reasserted central control over the levers of power within the country—the TV stations, the gas industry, the oil industry, the regions. It was a cunning feat of state rebuilding, aided by Putin's healthy contrast to the infirm Yeltsin, hyped fears of a Russian state dissolution, well-crafted appeals to patriotism, and the humbling of some oligarchs. Some fear of authority was necessary to tame the utter lawlessness into which the country had sunk. Putin instilled that fear, thanks to his own history and persona and some highhanded political theater, such as the arrest of Khodorkovsky, who was taken right off his private jet, which was shown again and again on Russian TV. But Putin's transformation into a dominant political figure required more than a widely shared appreciation that he was saving the Russian state. It also took a surprise economic boom.

From 1999 through 2008, Russia's economy grew at a brisk seven percent annually, thereby doubling its GDP in ruble terms. Real individual income growth was even brisker, increasing by two and a half times. In dollar terms, because of the ruble's appreciation over time, the increase in GDP was exceptionally vivid: from a nadir of around $196 billion in 1999 to around $2.1 trillion in 2013. A new, grateful Russian middle class was born, some 30 million strong, able to travel and shop abroad easily. More broadly, Russian society was transformed: cell-phone penetration went from zero to 100 percent, unemployment dropped from 12.9 percent to 6.3 percent, and the poverty rate fell from 29 percent to 13 percent. Wages rose, pensions were doled out, and the immense national debt that had been accumulated by previous leaders was paid off early. Foreign investors reaped rich rewards, too, as Russia's stock market skyrocketed, increasing 20-fold.

Many analysts have attributed the Russian boom to luck, in the form of plentiful fossil fuels. Yet although oil and gas have generally brought in approximately 50 percent of the Russian state's revenues, they have accounted for no more than 30 percent of the economy at large—a high number, but significantly lower than Middle East petrostate proportions. Even adding in all the knock-on effects around hydrocarbons, the most sophisticated analyses of Russian economic growth credit oil and gas with at most 40 to 50 percent of GDP during the boom. An immense amount of other value was created during these years as well, and Putin was partly responsible.

As president, Putin delegated handling of the economy to Mikhail Kasyanov, his prime minister; German Gref, the minister of economic development and trade; and Kudrin, then the finance minister, who introduced a raft of anti-inflationary and liberalizing measures (Gazprom excepted). Tax cuts increased incentives to work and reduced incentives to hide income. Simplification of business licensing and reduced inspections led to a burst of entrepreneurialism. Financial reforms and sensible macroeconomic policy facilitated investment. And land became a marketable commodity.

The impact of these pro-market reforms, which Putin supported and signed, was magnified by favorable trade winds. Russia had undergone a searing debt default and currency devaluation in 1998, and most commentators thought the country would be devastated. But in fact, the devaluation unintentionally made Russian exports cheaper and thus more competitive. At the same time, China's ongoing rise lifted global prices for Russian products, from fertilizer and chemicals to metals and cement. Insatiable Chinese demand brought Soviet legacy industries back from the dead. Brand-new sectors surged as well, such as retail, food processing, biotechnology, and software, driven by increased domestic demand and global outsourcing. Many of the Soviet legacy industries, such as coal and steel, underwent significant rationalization, as unprofitable mines or plants were phased out. (Agriculture, however, was never really revived, let alone rationalized, and Russia became dependent on food imports.)

Skeptics take note: oil prices during Putin's first presidential term, when growth was robust, averaged only around $35 a barrel; during Putin's second term, the average grew to around $65 a barrel. In recent years, with oil prices consistently at or above $100 a barrel, Russia's economy has stagnated.

China's rise, the ruble's devaluation, and a pent-up wave of structural reforms were critical to the Russian boom, but as the man in charge, Putin took the lion's share of the credit. His critics refuse to acknowledge his contribution, and some have improbably made him out to be a nonentity. In her 2012 biography, *The Man Without a Face*, for example, the Russian American journalist Masha Gessen offers the ultimate portrait of Putin as an accident. A well-written, impassioned compendium of facts, hearsay, and psychologizing about Putin's life and career, Gessen's book makes Putin out to be a mere thug and self-dealer, a murderer but ultimately a small man. Yet accidents and nonentities do not stay in power this long.

Mr. Putin, by Fiona Hill and Clifford Gaddy, two Russia hands at the Brookings Institution, offers less drama but more balance. It characterizes Putin as moving back and forth among six different personas: the Statist, the History Man (celebrating tsarist Russian statesmen), the Survivalist, the Outsider (not a Muscovite, not an apparatchik, not even a typical KGB officer), the Free Marketeer (actually, crony capitalist), and the Case Officer (who wins people's confidence through manipulation, bribery, and blackmail). It is a nicely rounded portrait. It is not, however, an intimate one.

Refreshingly, Hill and Gaddy refrain from imputing motives to Putin. They have met with him briefly in a large group but rely mostly on many of the same few voices that are quoted in Gessen's book, as well as in foundational biographies by Oleg Blotsky and Alexander Rahr, and on a published interview with the former Kremlin insider Gleb Pavlovsky. In their best chapters, Hill and Gaddy delineate the self-defeating cross-purposes among the six Putin personas, along with Putin's limitations when it comes to public politics. They rebut the prevalent American narrative about a tragic Putin betrayal of a Yeltsin-era trajectory toward democracy, bending over backward to make understandable the alternative Russian narrative of a Putin-led rescue from a 1990s "time of troubles." But they do not advance their own explicit, systematic explanation for how it was possible, in such a vast country, to establish what they dub a "one-boy network" political system.

FOLLOW THE MONEY

Western sanctions levied against Russia over its actions in Ukraine have targeted not economic sectors but individuals. *Putin's Kleptocracy*, by Karen Dawisha, shows why such an approach makes sense. It offers a comprehensive catalog of Putin's cronies: Arkady and Boris Rotenberg of gas pipeline construction fame, Gennady Timchenko of the Gunvor Group, Igor Sechin of Rosneft, Alexey Miller of Gazprom, Sergey Chemezov of Rosoboronexport, Yuri Kovalchuk of Bank Rossiya, Matthias Warnig of Nord Stream pipeline, and many more. Although a few of these individuals rose to power during the last decade and a half, most got to know Putin early, during his St. Petersburg years. (Warnig's relationship with Putin dates back to Dresden.) Dawisha details how they all got filthy rich thanks to the noncompetitive privatization of state assets, no-bid government contracts, dubious loans, fake bankruptcies, phantom middleman firms, tax "refunds," patriotic megaprojects (such as the Olympics), and other favors. She maintains that Putin, too, is a thief, and, calling attention to the $700,000 worth of watches publicly spotted on his wrist, she repeats guesstimates that put his personal wealth at $40 billion.

A political scientist at Miami University in Ohio, Dawisha has, for the most part, not uncovered new information but assembled in one place nuggets from the diplomatic cables published by WikiLeaks, investigative reportage, old Stasi files, comments made by an important Russian defector, and other sources, all of which she has posted online. Her prose is workmanlike, and not all the disparate materials fit easily into her simple storyline.

Particularly striking is the fact that most of the book is devoted to the period before Putin first became president. Dawisha reminds us that the KGB's role in private business began even before the Soviet collapse, and she argues that these are the roots of Putin's kleptocracy—challenging the conventional wisdom in which the 2003 arrest of Khodorkovsky and the confiscation of his private oil giant, Yukos, marked a key turning point. "Like other scholars of Russia, I have spent a significant portion of my career thinking and writing about how the post-Communist states might make a transition toward democracy," she confesses, but says that eventually she got wise, concluding that Russia was not "an inchoate democratic system being pulled down by history, accidental autocrats, popular inertia, bureaucratic incompetence, or poor Western advice." Rather, "from the beginning Putin and his circle sought to create an authoritarian regime ruled by a close-knit cabal with embedded interests, plans, and capabilities, who used democracy for decoration rather than direction." Putin's nasty tendencies, in other words, cannot be blamed on external factors, such as NATO expansion.

Questions about her analysis can be raised. Dawisha never really clarifies, for example, the extent to which sincerely held beliefs bind the Putin kleptocrats (as they did, say, the old Brezhnev clique, who also were said to be a bunch of cynics). She quotes Nikolay Leonov, the former head of analysis for the KGB, as saying of Putin and his

KGB associates back in 2001, "They are patriots and proponents of a strong state grounded in centuries-old tradition. History recruited them to carry out a special operation for the resurrection of our great power, because there has to be balance in the world, and without a strong Russia the geopolitical turbulence will begin." So is the enrichment an end in itself or a means to an end?

Most fundamentally, Dawisha's assertions about near-total intentionality—kleptocracy by "intelligent design"—strain credulity. Russia has known lots of designs, including those of Mikhail Gorbachev and Yeltsin, and what happened to them? She concedes that under Putin, "not everything went as planned," but her telling of the story makes it seem otherwise. This misses the fact that Putin and his cronies, as well as his mass base, were largely losers under Gorbachev and Yeltsin. Notwithstanding its private-sector and off-shore machinations, the former KGB was initially cut out of the really big money in oil, gas, metals, diamonds, and gold. A strong continuity argument obscures the shifts and contingencies that have occurred, as well as the progressive radicalization in the kleptocracy that has taken place over time—not only after 2003 but even over the last two years. Dawisha also overlooks any dynamic beyond Putin. Property is continually being expropriated by regime loyalists because that is a major way they mark their relative status in the pecking order—and how they survive, warding off attacks from others by going on offensive raids themselves.

Dawisha's portrait of Putin's supposed primordial will to enrichment leads her to dismiss not just his first-term structural reforms and the vision behind them but also the four-year presidential term of his junior crony, Dmitry Medvedev—an episode that followed Putin's decision to respect, at least formally, the constitutional limit of two consecutive presidential terms. The dismissal may be understandable: Medvedev was (and is) derisively known as "the Teddy Bear" (*Medvezhonok*). He was picked for a reason. And yet throughout his tenure, Medvedev was urged by his own entourage and various powerful interest groups to dismiss Putin from the prime ministership.

One can debate the seriousness of the Medvedev-approved investigation of the Kremlin's own Khodorkovsky prosecution, the pressure campaign against Sechin and other Putin cronies serving on the boards of private companies, the timid moves toward economic diversification and redemocratization, and the improved relations with the United States. One could even implausibly assume that all of that was brilliant manipulation by remarkably clever and effective puppet masters in order to fool the Russian people and the West. But the fact remains that Medvedev had full authority to dismiss Putin, to deny him access to state resources in a campaign, and to declare his own intention to run for reelection. That the Teddy Bear did not make a move does not mean he couldn't have.

EMPEROR WITHOUT CLOTHES

In *Fragile Empire*, the journalist Ben Judah sees Putin's return to the presidency for a third term as a severe blow to the regime. His punchy book can be flip, but he talked to so many people, and lets their voices be heard, that his own snark and contempt are somewhat offset. "You see this man had good qualities, too," Alexander Belyaev, the former head of the St. Petersburg city assembly, tells him of Putin. "He was an expert at making friends, of being loyal to those friends. He is a brilliant observer of human nature, and he is very good at tactics." Similarly, Sergei Kolesnikov, a member of Putin's St. Petersburg clique who had been helping finance a palace for Putin in the south before choosing to expose his corruption and then going into exile in Estonia, tells Judah, "I was surprised when Putin became president. Of course I was surprised, everyone was surprised. At first I really wanted to support him and help him in any way I could. The 1990s had been a criminal, dangerous time. I hoped for something different." The something different turned out to be a personal dictatorship.

Judah has actually written two books. One is about what he calls Putin's "telepopulism," in which he discusses the Kremlin's spin doctors and puppeteers, such as Vladislav Surkov, and how the George W. Bush administration's aggressions and transgressions proved to be a gift to their manipulations. But the concept of the Putin regime as a "videocracy" dead ends, because, as Judah himself demonstrates, the propaganda is not always so effective and Putinism is more than mere show; it is a society. Judah details how Russian state spending on security, law, and order went from $2.8 billion in 2000 to $36.5 billion by 2010. More than 40 percent of the new middle class works for the state, and therefore they are not independent people. The regime's social base, in other words, is itself.

The other book is a vivid portrait of Moscow as an oppressive colonial power in its own lands. Judah travels out to remote locales and finds the little Putins, the feudal lords presiding over near state-lessness and profound despair. He makes it to desolate Tuva, once part of Mongolia, in southern Siberia, where Putin is said to have posed topless for the cameras on a faux hunting expedition. "Putin?" a villager from Erjei says to the author. "He never did anything good for the country. He just took all the money from oil and gas production and took it for himself and his mates. . . . Why the hell would we support Putin?" Judah also travels to Birobidzhan, the improbable Soviet Jewish homeland on the border with China, and finds no sign of a feared Chinese demographic invasion. "Are you worried that in the future the land will not be Russian and will be controlled by China? That there will be no more motherland here?" he asks mushroom sellers in a Russian area leased to Chinese farmers who grow soybeans. "Who gives a fuck about the motherland," the mushroom sellers answer. "There is no fucking motherland."

How representative such interviews are remains unclear. Judah apparently spent little time in Russia's many bustling provincial cities, such as Yekaterinburg, Novosibirsk, or Lipetsk, which are clearly better off today than they were even just a few years ago. His reporting is designed not to offer a full picture of Russia but to show how the lawlessness Putin sought to fix is worse than ever. He finds the predominantly Muslim North Caucasus, a place where Putin pays colossal tribute for a sheen of loyalty, nearly fully de-Russified. Whereas previously it was the Chechens who wanted out of Russia,

Judah writes, now many Russians would not mind seeing Chechnya go, since they detest the massive budget transfers to the region ($30 billion for nine million inhabitants between 2000 and 2010).

Judah has some smart things to say about the Russian Internet, pointing out that "unlike in other Eastern European countries, the platforms that hosted it were largely indigenous because of the Cyrillic script, allowing it to become a 'pole' in the emerging online world, like China, which also uses home-grown platforms." Russian equivalents for Google and Facebook, moreover, have operated largely beyond the suffocating regime. "The Internet grew in Russia in a kind of utopia—where there was no state," one interviewee tells Judah. "This was the only part of the economy where to be a player and to be a winner you needed no political connections, no United Russia membership card, and no visits to the Kremlin." All that has been changing, however, since the book was written.

Judah rips into the Internet-savvy opposition to Putin for being out of touch with the common people. He describes Alexei Navalny, the blogger who rose to fame as a critic of corruption, as a xenophobe and a "pure product of Putinism." Judah heaps disdain on the tens of thousands of Muscovites who risked going out into the streets in 2011–12 to protest the regime, calling them "the demographic in Russia . . . most accustomed to skiing in France" and asserting that "the protests failed because Moscow is not Russia." (Protests occurred in many cities.) His condescension descends into incoherence when he writes of Pussy Riot, the punk band that carried out an ill-fated performance act in an Orthodox church, that they "captured the vanity and, ironically, the unpolitical nature of the radical art scene. They were interested in protest, not politics." Readers are likely to find this an often engaging book marred by an excess of attitude.

Still, Judah offers one of the best accounts of how Putin built his personal regime out of the mundane process of addressing the pathologies of the Russian state he inherited. To clean things up, an undertaking for which Putin had wide support, he had to acquire ever more power. All the while, a bogeyman served him well—not a return to communism, Yeltsin's scarecrow, but the chaos of Yeltsinism. "The power to control the Russian nightmare of total collapse brought [Putin] to power and has kept him in power," Judah succinctly summarizes.

But none of this unfolded automatically; the construction of such a regime required certain skills and real work. Putin seized an opportunity provided by historical contingencies, and he proved up to the task. He made himself indispensable to all factions and interests, their guarantor—or not—in a system in which uncertainty besets even the richest and most powerful. He shamelessly monetized his political position, but he also turned out to be dedicated to the cause of Russian statehood, in his own KGB way. Certain kinds of leaders do seem to fit certain moments in a country's history. Putin only looks like an accident. And it is precisely because he is not a nonentity that he has been a calamity.

THE LONELY POWER

Remarkably, this pattern keeps repeating itself in Russia. About a decade ago, Stefan Hedlund, an expert on Russia at Uppsala University, in Sweden, wrote an impressive overview of 12 centuries of Eastern Slavic history in an attempt to explain Putin's authoritarianism. He pointed out that Russia had essentially collapsed three times—in 1610–13, 1917–18, and 1991—and that each time, the country was revived fundamentally unchanged. Despite the depth of the crises and the stated intentions of would-be transformative leaders, Russia reemerged with an unaccountable government, repression, and resistance to the imposition of the rule of law. Hedlund's impressive tome was titled *Russian Path Dependence*, but rather than complete determinism, he perceived choices—albeit choices heavily conditioned by culture. He noted that efforts at institutional change in Russia had always failed because they had not altered the country's underlying system of norms, which rested on a deeply ingrained preference for informal rules. "Modernization reinforced archaism," Hedlund grimly concluded, quoting the historian Geoffrey Hosking; "increasing state control meant entrenching personal caprice."

Hedlund's attention to values yielded exceptional insight, but he overemphasized the institutional continuities supposedly at work from ancient Muscovy onward and underplayed the power of Russia's relations with the outside world. Not just a preference for informal rules but also Russia's quest for great-power status, and especially its perennial difficulties competing with stronger powers, has produced both the collapses and the trying aftermaths, during which an imperative to revive national greatness comes to the fore. "Russia was and will remain a great power," announced Putin's original presidential manifesto, posted online in late 1999. "Russia is in the middle of one of the most difficult periods in its history. For the first time in the past 200–300 years, it is facing a real threat of sliding into the second, possibly even the third, echelon of states." In response, he offered an abiding vision of Russia as a providential power, with a special mission and distinct identity. Exceptionalism has been the handmaiden of personalism.

Putin resembles a villain out of central casting. He has repeatedly revealed himself as cocksure, patronizing, aggrieved, vindictive, and quick with a retort for Western critics. But he is hardly the first Russian leader to make demonization of the West a foundation of Russia's core identity and its government's claim to legitimacy. Moreover, today's Russia is significantly more ethnically homogeneous and nationalist than was the old Soviet Union, and Putin has perfected the art of moistening the eyes of Russian elites assembled in opulent tsarist settings, plucking the strings of mystical pride in all things Russian and of ressentiment at all things Western. They see reason where critics see madness. From the Kremlin's perspective, as Washington engages in stupid, hypocritical, and destabilizing global behavior, Moscow shoulders the burden of serving as a counterweight, thereby bringing sanity and balance to the international system. Russian lying, cheating, and hypocrisy thus serve a higher purpose. Cybercrime is patriotism; rigging elections and demobilizing opposition are sacred duties. Putin's machismo posturing, additionally, is undergirded by a view of Russia as a country of real men opposing a pampered, gutless, and decadent West. Resentment toward U.S. power resonates far beyond Russia, and with his ramped-up social conservatism, Putin has expanded a perennial sense of Russian exceptionalism to include an alternative social model as well.

Paradoxically, however, all of this has only helped render Russia what the analyst Lilia Shevtsova has aptly called a "lonely power." Putin's predatory politics at home and abroad, his cozying up to right-wing extremists in Europe, and his attempted engagement of a powerful China hardly add up to an effective Russian grand strategy. Russia has no actual allies and has damaged its most important relationship, that with Germany. Winning domestic plaudits at Western powers' expense is politically useful, but those countries, as always, continue to possess the advanced technology Russia needs, especially in energy exploration and drilling. Over the long term, realizing the ambitions Putin and his supporters have articulated would require new and deeper structural reforms, a dramatic cutback in bureaucracy and state procurement shenanigans, and the creation of an environment supportive of entrepreneurialism and investment. Medvedev made gestures in such a direction, but Putin has ridiculed those, choosing the path of least resistance in the short term and thus risking possible long-term stagnation or worse. A revival of Russia's latent Soviet-era industrial capacity was a trick that could happen only once.

Emotive nationalism and social conservatism have long been present in post-Soviet Russia, but they have intensified in state propaganda since 2012. This was due partly to the outbreak of street protests in the winter of 2011–12 challenging Putin's announcement that he would return to the presidency. But more fundamentally, it was also because the other possible way forward—a second round of structural reform—would have been incredibly hard to carry out, not least because it might have threatened to undermine the current elite's suffocating grasp on power. As it happened, the mass Ukrainian uprising against misrule that began in late 2013 and culminated in President Viktor Yanukovych's cowardly abandonment of Kiev in February 2014 reconfirmed the long-standing Kremlin line of a scheming West committed to encircling and overthrowing the regime in Russia. Putin's seizure of the southern Ukrainian region of Crimea, in turn, strongly reinforced the trend in the Kremlin away from facing the tough policy choices that would actually bolster Russia's great-power status.

Given the West's imposition of sanctions and dropping world oil prices, it might be tempting to write Putin off. Authoritarian regimes often prove to be at once all-powerful and strikingly brittle, and Judah, for one, sees Putin's rule as almost on its last legs. And yet, despite the Russian population's seething anger over its predatory state and educated urbanites' despondency over the absence of a modernizing vision for the future, much of the elite retains a strong sense of mission and resolve. Dawisha concludes that "Putin will not go gentle into the night," and she is probably correct. Judah underestimates the ways this new kind of flexible authoritarianism has found to adapt to often self-created challenges, and his book is bereft of any discussion of foreign policy, a vital instrument in the tool kit of authoritarianism.

Putin's Russia possesses powerful resources as a potential international spoiler, including the ability to apply economic pressure, buy off or co-opt powerful foreign interests, engage in covert operations, wage cyberattacks, and deploy a modernizing military force that is by far the strongest in the region. Ironically, Russia's greatest source of leverage might be the fact that the West, especially Europe, needs its neighbor's integration into the international order. Managing such integration would be a lot less difficult if Putin were just a thief, à la Dawisha, or a cynic, à la Judah. But he is actually a composite, à la Hill and Gaddy—a thief and a cynic with deeply held convictions about the special qualities and mission of the Russian state, views that enjoy wide resonance among the population. So what happens now, especially given that the Russian leader has managed to trap himself in the latest and largest of his so-called frozen conflicts, enraging the West and setting himself on a path toward isolation and creeping autarky?

A WAY OUT?

Neither Putin nor his Western counterparts planned to get embroiled in a prolonged standoff over Ukraine. Russia's seizure of Crimea and support for separatist rebels in eastern Ukraine violated international law and, following the downing of a civilian airliner (almost certainly by Russian-assisted rebels), provoked the imposition of significant Western sanctions. But the crisis is not simply about Russian aggression, nor can it be solved simply by trying to force Moscow to retreat to the status quo ante. Even an unlikely retreat, moreover, would not necessarily last.

Ukraine is a debilitated state, created under Soviet auspices, hampered by a difficult Soviet inheritance, and hollowed out by its own predatory elites during two decades of misrule. But it is also a nation that is too big and independent for Russia to swallow up. Russia, meanwhile, is a damaged yet still formidable great power whose rulers cannot be intimidated into allowing Ukraine to enter the Western orbit. Hence the standoff. No external power or aid package can solve Ukraine's problems or compensate for its inherent vulnerabilities vis-à-vis Russia. Nor would sending lethal weaponry to Ukraine's brave but ragtag volunteer fighters and corrupt state structures improve the situation; in fact, it would send it spiraling further downward, by failing to balance Russian predominance while giving Moscow a pretext to escalate the conflict even more. Rather, the way forward must begin with a recognition of some banal facts and some difficult bargaining.

Russia's seizure of Crimea and intervention in eastern Ukraine do not challenge the entire post-1945 international order. The forward positions the Soviet Union occupied in the heart of Europe as a result of defeating Nazi Germany were voluntarily relinquished in the early 1990s, and they are not going to be reoccupied. But nor should every detail of the post–Cold War settlement worked out in 1989–91 be considered eternal and inviolate. That settlement emerged during an anomalous time. Russia was flat on its back but would not remain prostrate forever, and when it recovered, some sort of pushback was to be expected.

Something similar happened following the Treaty of Versailles of 1919, many of the provisions of which were not enforced. Even if France, the United Kingdom, and the United States had been willing and able to enforce the peace, their efforts would not have worked, because the treaty had been imposed during a temporary anomaly, the simultaneous collapse of German and Russian power, and would inevitably have been challenged when that power returned.

Territorial revisionism ensued after World War II as well, of course, and continued sporadically for decades. Since 1991, there have been some negotiated revisions: Hong Kong and Macao underwent peaceful reabsorption into China. Yugoslavia was broken up in violence and war, leading to the independence of its six federal units and eventually Kosovo, as well. Unrecognized statelets such as Nagorno-Karabakh, part of Azerbaijan; Transnistria, a sliver of Moldova; Abkhazia and South Ossetia, disputed units of Georgia; and now Donetsk and Luhansk, parts of Ukraine—each entails a story of Stalinist border-making.

The European Union cannot resolve this latest standoff, nor can the United Nations. The United States has indeed put together "coalitions of the willing" to legitimize some of its recent interventions, but it is not going to go to war over Ukraine or start bombing Russia, and the wherewithal and will for indefinite sanctions against Russia are lacking. Distasteful as it might sound, Washington faces the prospect of trying to work out some negotiated larger territorial settlement.

Such negotiations would have to acknowledge that Russia is a great power with leverage, but they would not need to involve the formal acceptance of some special Russian sphere of interest in its so-called near abroad. The chief goals would be, first, to exchange international recognition of Russia's annexation of Crimea for an end to all the frozen conflicts in which Russia is an accomplice and, second, to disincentivize such behavior in the future. Russia should have to pay monetary compensation for Crimea. There could be some federal solutions, referendums, even land swaps and population transfers (which in many cases have already taken place). Sanctions on Russia would remain in place until a settlement was mutually agreed on, and new sanctions could be levied if Russia were to reject negotiations or were deemed to be conducting them in bad faith. Recognition of the new status of Crimea would occur in stages, over an extended period.

It would be a huge challenge to devise incentives that were politically plausible in the West while at the same time powerful enough for Russia to agree to a just settlement—and for Ukraine to be willing to take part. But the search for a settlement would be an opportunity as well as a headache.

NATO expansion can be judged to have been a strategic error—not because it angered Russia but because it weakened NATO as a military alliance. Russia's elites would likely have become revanchist even without NATO's advance, because they believe, nearly universally, that the United States took advantage of Russia in 1991 and has denied the country its rightful place as an equal in international diplomacy ever since. But NATO expansion's critics have not offered much in the way of practicable alternatives. Would it really have been appropriate, for example, to deny the requests of all the countries east of Germany to join the alliance?

Then as now, the only real alternative was the creation of an entirely new trans-European security architecture, one that fully transcended its Cold War counterpart. This was an oft-expressed Russian wish, but in the early 1990s, there was neither the imagination nor the incentives in Washington for such a heavy lift. Whether there is such capacity in Washington today remains to be seen. But even if comprehensive new security arrangements are unlikely anytime soon, Washington could still undertake much useful groundwork.

Critics might object on the grounds that the sanctions are actually biting, reinforced by the oil price free fall—so why offer even minimal concessions to Putin now? The answer is because neither the sanctions, nor the oil price collapse, nor the two in conjunction have altered Russia's behavior, diminished its potential as a spoiler, or afforded Ukraine a chance to recover.

Whether they acknowledge it or not, Western opponents of a negotiated settlement are really opting for another long-term, open-ended attempt to contain Russia and hope for regime change—a policy likely to last until the end of Putin's life and possibly well beyond. The costs of such an approach are likely to be quite high, and other global issues will continue to demand attention and resources. And all the while, Ukraine would effectively remain crippled, Europe's economy would suffer, and Russia would grow ever more embittered and difficult to handle. All of that might occur no matter what. But if negotiations hold out a chance of somehow averting such an outcome, they are worth a try. And the attempt would hold few costs, because failed negotiations would only solidify the case for containment in Europe and in the United States.

It is ultimately up to Russia's leaders to take meaningful steps to integrate their country into the existing world order, one that they can vex but not fully overturn. To the extent that the Ukraine debacle has brought this reality into sharper focus, it might actually have been useful in helping Putin to see some light, and the same goes for the collapse of oil prices and the accompanying unavoidable devaluation of the ruble. After the nadir of 1998, smart policy choices in Moscow, together with some lucky outside breaks, helped Russia transform a crisis into a breakthrough, with real and impressive steps forward. That history could replay itself—but whether it will remains the prerogative of one person alone.

Obama's Libya Debacle

How a Well-Meaning Intervention Ended in Failure

Alan J. Kuperman

AHMED JADALLAH / COURTESY REUTERS

Protesters chant slogans during a rally against former militia fighters in Tripoli, November 2013.

O n March 17, 2011, the UN Security Council passed Resolution 1973, spearheaded by the administration of U.S. President Barack Obama, authorizing military intervention in

ALAN J. KUPERMAN is an Associate Professor at the Lyndon B. Johnson School of Public Affairs at the University of Texas at Austin and the editor of *Constitutions and Conflict Management in Africa: Preventing Civil War Through Institutional Design.*

Libya. The goal, Obama explained, was to save the lives of peaceful, pro-democracy protesters who found themselves the target of a crackdown by Libyan dictator Muammar al-Qaddafi. Not only did Qaddafi endanger the momentum of the nascent Arab Spring, which had recently swept away authoritarian regimes in Tunisia and Egypt, but he also was poised to commit a bloodbath in the Libyan city where the uprising had started, said the president. "We knew that if we waited one more day, Benghazi—a city nearly the size of Charlotte—could suffer a massacre that would have reverberated across the region and stained the conscience of the world," Obama declared. Two days after the UN authorization, the United States and other NATO countries established a no-fly zone throughout Libya and started bombing Qaddafi's forces. Seven months later, in October 2011, after an extended military campaign with sustained Western support, rebel forces conquered the country and shot Qaddafi dead.

In the immediate wake of the military victory, U.S. officials were triumphant. Writing in these pages in 2012, Ivo Daalder, then the U.S. permanent representative to NATO, and James Stavridis, then supreme allied commander of Europe, declared, "NATO's operation in Libya has rightly been hailed as a model intervention." In the Rose Garden after Qaddafi's death, Obama himself crowed, "Without putting a single U.S. service member on the ground, we achieved our objectives." Indeed, the United States seemed to have scored a hat trick: nurturing the Arab Spring, averting a Rwanda-like genocide, and eliminating Libya as a potential source of terrorism.

That verdict, however, turns out to have been premature. In retrospect, Obama's intervention in Libya was an abject failure, judged even by its own standards. Libya has not only failed to evolve into a democracy; it has devolved into a failed state. Violent deaths and other human rights abuses have increased severalfold. Rather than helping the United States combat terrorism, as Qaddafi did during his last decade in power, Libya now serves as a safe haven for militias affiliated with both al Qaeda and the Islamic

State of Iraq and al-Sham (ISIS). The Libya intervention has harmed other U.S. interests as well: undermining nuclear nonproliferation, chilling Russian cooperation at the UN, and fueling Syria's civil war.

Despite what defenders of the mission claim, there was a better policy available—not intervening at all, because peaceful Libyan civilians were not actually being targeted. Had the United States and its allies followed that course, they could have spared Libya from the resulting chaos and given it a chance of progress under Qaddafi's chosen successor: his relatively liberal, Western-educated son Saif al-Islam. Instead, Libya today is riddled with vicious militias and anti-American terrorists—and thus serves as a cautionary tale of how humanitarian intervention can backfire for both the intervener and those it is intended to help.

A FAILED STATE

Optimism about Libya reached its apogee in July 2012, when democratic elections brought to power a moderate, secular coalition government—a stark change from Qaddafi's four decades of dictatorship. But the country quickly slid downhill. Its first elected prime minister, Mustafa Abu Shagour, lasted less than one month in office. His quick ouster foreshadowed the trouble to come: as of this writing, Libya has had seven prime ministers in less than four years. Islamists came to dominate the first postwar parliament, the General National Congress. Meanwhile, the new government failed to disarm dozens of militias that had arisen during NATO's seven-month intervention, especially Islamist ones, leading to deadly turf battles between rival tribes and commanders, which continue to this day. In October 2013, secessionists in eastern Libya, where most of the country's oil is located, declared their own government. That same month, Ali Zeidan, then the country's prime minister, was kidnapped and held hostage. In light of the growing Islamist influence within Libya's government, in the spring of 2014, the United States postponed a plan to train an armed force of 6,000–8,000 Libyan troops.

By May 2014, Libya had come to the brink of a new civil war—between liberals and Islamists. That month, a renegade secular general named Khalifa Hifter seized control of the air force to attack Islamist militias in Benghazi, later expanding his targets to include the Islamist-dominated legislature in Tripoli. Elections last June did nothing to resolve the chaos. Most Libyans had already given up on democracy, as voter turnout dropped from 1.7 million in the previous poll to just 630,000. Secular parties declared victory and formed a new legislature, the House of Representatives, but the Islamists refused to accept that outcome. The result was two competing parliaments, each claiming to be the legitimate one.

In July, an Islamist militia from the city of Misurata responded to Hifter's actions by attacking Tripoli, prompting Western embassies to evacuate. After a six-week battle, the Islamists captured the capital in August on behalf of the so-called Libya Dawn coalition, which, together with the defunct legislature, formed what they labeled a "national salvation government." In October, the newly elected parliament, led by the secular Operation Dignity coalition, fled to the eastern city of Tobruk, where it established a competing interim government, which Libya's Supreme Court later declared unconstitutional. Libya thus finds itself with two warring governments, each controlling only a fraction of the country's territory and militias.

As bad as Libya's human rights situation was under Qaddafi, it has gotten worse since NATO ousted him. Immediately after taking power, the rebels perpetrated scores of reprisal killings, in addition to torturing, beating, and arbitrarily detaining thousands of suspected Qaddafi supporters. The rebels also expelled 30,000 mostly black residents from the town of Tawergha and burned or looted their homes and shops, on the grounds that some of them supposedly had been mercenaries. Six months after the war, Human Rights Watch declared that the abuses "appear to be so widespread and systematic that they may amount to crimes against humanity."

Such massive violations persist. In October 2013, the UN Office of the High Commissioner for Human Rights reported that the "vast majority of the estimated 8,000 conflict-related detainees are also being held without due process." More disturbing, Amnesty International issued a report last year that revealed their savage mistreatment: "Detainees were subjected to prolonged beatings with plastic tubes, sticks, metal bars or cables. In some cases, they were subjected to electric shocks, suspended in contorted positions for hours, kept continuously blindfolded and shackled with their hands tied behind their backs or deprived of food and water." The report also noted some 93 attacks on Libyan journalists in just the first nine months of 2014, "including abductions, arbitrary arrests, assassinations, assassination attempts and assaults." Ongoing attacks in western Libya, the report concluded, "amount to war crimes." As a consequence of such pervasive violence, the UN estimates that roughly 400,000 Libyans have fled their homes, a quarter of whom have left the country altogether.

Libya's quality of life has been sharply degraded by an economic free fall. That is mainly because the country's production of oil, its lifeblood, remains severely depressed by the protracted conflict. Prior to the revolution, Libya produced 1.65 million barrels of oil a day, a figure that dropped to zero during NATO's intervention. Although production temporarily recovered to 85 percent of its previous rate, ever since secessionists seized eastern oil ports in August 2013, output has averaged only 30 percent of the prewar level. Ongoing fighting has closed airports and seaports in Libya's two biggest cities, Tripoli and Benghazi. In many cities, residents are subjected to massive power outages—up to 18 hours a day in Tripoli. The recent privation represents a stark descent for a country that the UN's Human Development Index traditionally had ranked as having the highest standard of living in all of Africa.

THE HUMAN COST

Although the White House justified its mission in Libya on humanitarian grounds, the intervention in fact greatly magnified the death toll there. To begin with, Qaddafi's crackdown turns out to have been much less lethal than media reports indicated at the time. In eastern Libya, where the uprising began as a mix of peaceful and violent protests, Human Rights Watch documented only 233 deaths in the first days of the fighting, not 10,000, as had been reported by the Saudi news channel Al Arabiya. In fact, as I documented in a 2013 *International Security* article, from mid-February 2011, when the rebellion started, to mid-March 2011, when NATO intervened, only about 1,000 Libyans died, including soldiers and rebels. Although an Al Jazeera article touted by Western media in early 2011 alleged that Qaddafi's air force had strafed and bombed civilians in Benghazi and Tripoli, "the story was untrue," revealed an exhaustive examination in the *London Review of Books* by Hugh Roberts of Tufts University. Indeed, striving to minimize civilian casualties, Qaddafi's forces had refrained from indiscriminate violence.

The best statistical evidence of that comes from Misurata, Libya's third-largest city, where the initial fighting raged most intensely. Human Rights Watch found that of the 949 people wounded there in the rebellion's first seven weeks, only 30 (just over three percent) were women or children, which indicates that Qaddafi's forces had narrowly targeted combatants, who were virtually all male. During that same period in Misurata, only 257 people were killed, a tiny fraction of the city's 400,000 residents.

The same pattern of restraint was evident in Tripoli, where the government used significant force for only two days prior to NATO's intervention, to beat back violent protesters who were burning government buildings. Libyan doctors subsequently told a UN investigative commission that they observed more than 200 corpses in the city's morgues on February 20–21 but that only two of them were female. These statistics refute the notion that Qaddafi's forces fired indiscriminately at peaceful civilians.

Moreover, by the time NATO intervened, Libya's violence was on the verge of ending. Qaddafi's well-armed forces had routed the ragtag rebels, who were retreating home. By mid-March 2011, government forces were poised to recapture the last rebel stronghold of Benghazi, thereby ending the one-month conflict at a total cost of just over 1,000 lives. Just then, however, Libyan expatriates in Switzerland affiliated with the rebels issued warnings of an impending "bloodbath" in Benghazi, which Western media duly reported but which in retrospect appear to have been propaganda. In reality, on March 17, Qaddafi pledged to protect the civilians of Benghazi, as he had those of other recaptured cities, adding that his forces had "left the way open" for the rebels to retreat to Egypt. Simply put, the militants were about to lose the war, and so their overseas agents raised the specter of genocide to attract a NATO intervention—which worked like a charm. There is no evidence or reason to believe that Qaddafi had planned or intended to perpetrate a killing campaign.

Admittedly, the government did attempt to intimidate the rebels, promising to pursue them relentlessly. But Qaddafi never translated that rhetoric into targeting civilians. From March 5 to March 15, 2011, government forces recaptured all but one of the major rebel-held cities, and in none did they kill civilians in revenge, let alone commit a bloodbath. Indeed, as his forces approached Benghazi, Qaddafi issued public reassurances that they would harm neither civilians nor rebels who disarmed. On March 17, he directly addressed the rebels of Benghazi: "Throw away your weapons, exactly like your brothers in Ajdabiya and other places did. They laid down their arms and they are safe. We never pursued them at all."

Two days later, however, the NATO air campaign halted Qaddafi's offensive. As a result, Benghazi did not return to government control, the rebels did not flee, and the war did not end. Instead, the militants reversed their retreat and went back on the offensive. Eventually, on October 20, 2011, the rebels found Qaddafi, tortured him, and then summarily executed him. The regime's last remnants fell three days later. All told, the intervention extended Libya's civil war from less than six weeks to more than eight months.

Claims of the number killed during the war have varied wildly. At a closed-door conference in November 2011 organized by the Brookings Institution, one U.S. official characterized the final death toll as "around 8,000." By contrast, the rebels' health minister asserted in September 2011, before the war was even over, that 30,000 Libyans had already died. However, the postwar government's Ministry of Martyrs and Missing Persons sharply reduced that figure to 4,700 civilians and rebels, plus an equal or lesser number of regime forces, and 2,100 people missing on both sides—for a high-end death estimate of 11,500.

Aggregate casualty statistics were not compiled during the subsequent two years of persistent low-level conflict, but reports did emerge of several significant skirmishes, such as a March 2012 fight between rival tribes in the southern city of Sabha that left 147 dead. In light of such figures, it is reasonable to estimate that the conflict killed at least 500 people a year in 2012 and 2013. Better data are available for the renewed civil war of 2014. The website Libya Body Count, which documents casualties daily, reports that the total number of Libyans killed last year was more than 2,750. Moreover, unlike Qaddafi's forces in 2011, the militias fighting in Libya today do use force indiscriminately. In August 2014, for example, the Tripoli Medical Center reported that of the 100 killed in recent violence, 40 were women and at least nine were children. The following month, in a blatant war crime, militants fired a multiple-rocket launcher at a medical facility.

This grim math leads to a depressing but unavoidable conclusion. Before NATO's intervention, Libya's civil war was on the verge of ending, at the cost of barely 1,000 lives. Since then, however, Libya has suffered at least 10,000 additional deaths from conflict. In other words, NATO's intervention appears to have increased the violent death toll more than tenfold.

TERRITORY FOR TERRORISTS

Another unintended consequence of the Libya intervention has been to amplify the threat of terrorism from the country. Although Qaddafi supported terrorism decades ago—as witnessed by his regime's later paying reparations for the Lockerbie airplane bombing of 1988—the Libyan leader had evolved into a U.S. ally against global terrorism even before 9/11. He did so partly because he faced a domestic threat from al Qaeda–affiliated militants, the Libyan Islamic Fighting Group. Qaddafi's external security chief, Moussa Koussa, met multiple times with senior CIA officials to provide intelligence about Libyan fighters in Afghanistan and about the Pakistani nuclear peddler A. Q. Khan. In 2009, General William Ward, who headed U.S. Africa Command, praised Libya as "a top partner in combating transnational terrorism."

Since NATO's intervention in 2011, however, Libya and its neighbor Mali have turned into terrorist havens. Radical Islamist groups, which Qaddafi had suppressed, emerged under NATO air cover as some of the most competent fighters of the rebellion. Supplied with weapons by sympathetic countries such as Qatar, the militias refused to disarm after Qaddafi fell. Their persistent threat was highlighted in September 2012 when jihadists, including from the group Ansar al-Sharia, attacked the U.S. diplomatic compound in Benghazi, killing Christopher Stevens, the U.S. ambassador to Libya, and three of his colleagues. Last year, the UN formally declared Ansar al-Sharia a terrorist organization because of its affiliation with al Qaeda in the Islamic Maghreb.

Libya's Islamist militants are now fighting for control of the entire country, and they are making headway. In April 2014, they captured a secret military base near Tripoli that, ironically, U.S. special operations forces had established in the summer of 2012 to train Libyan counterterrorist forces. Qatar and Sudan have flown weapons to the Islamists as recently as September 2014. In response, the more secular governments of the United Arab Emirates and Egypt launched air strikes against Islamist militants in Tripoli and Benghazi in August and October of last year. Libya's jihadists now include more than just al Qaeda affiliates; as of January 2015, factions aligned with ISIS, also known as the Islamic State, have perpetrated killings or kidnappings in all three of Libya's traditional administrative zones.

NATO's intervention also fostered Islamist terrorism elsewhere in the region. When Qaddafi fell, the ethnic Tuaregs of Mali within his security forces fled home with their weapons to launch their own rebellion. That uprising was quickly hijacked by local Islamist forces and al Qaeda in the Islamic Maghreb, which declared an independent Islamic state in Mali's northern half. By December 2012, this zone of Mali had become "the largest territory controlled by Islamic extremists in the world," according to Senator Christopher Coons, chair of the U.S. Senate Subcommittee on Africa. The danger was elaborated by *The New York Times*, which reported that "al Qaeda's affiliate in North Africa is operating terrorist training camps in northern Mali and providing arms, explosives and financing to a militant Islamist organization in northern Nigeria." But the spillover from Libya did not stop there, also spurring deadly ethnic conflict in Burkina Faso and the growth of radical Islam in Niger. To contain this threat, in early 2013, France was compelled to deploy thousands of troops to Mali, some of whom continue to fight jihadists in the country's north.

The terrorism problem was exacerbated by the leakage of sensitive weapons from Qaddafi's arsenal to radical Islamists across North Africa and the Middle East. Peter Bouckaert of Human Rights Watch estimates that ten times as many weapons went loose in Libya as in Somalia, Afghanistan, or Iraq. Perhaps the greatest concern is man-portable air defense systems, known as MANPADs, which in capable hands can be used to shoot down both civilian airliners and military aircraft. Up to 15,000 such missiles were unaccounted for as of February 2012, according to a U.S. State Department official cited in a *Washington Post* column; a $40 million buyback effort had secured only 5,000 of them. The column added that hundreds of these weapons were still on the loose, including in Niger, where some had been obtained by Boko Haram, the radical Islamist group across the border in northern Nigeria. Another few dozen have been found in Algeria and Egypt.

The missiles have even made their way through Egypt to the Gaza Strip. In October 2012, militants there fired one for the first time, just missing an Israeli army helicopter, and Israeli officials said that the weapons originated in Libya. More recently, in early 2014, Islamists in Egypt used another such missile to shoot down a military helicopter. Libyan MANPADs and sea mines have even surfaced in West African arms markets, where Somali buyers have snapped them up for Islamist rebels and pirates far away in northeastern Africa.

THE BROADER BACKLASH

The harm from the intervention in Libya extends well beyond the immediate neighborhood. For one thing, by helping overthrow Qaddafi, the United States undercut its own nuclear nonproliferation objectives. In 2003, Qaddafi had voluntarily halted his nuclear and chemical weapons programs and surrendered his arsenals to the United States. His reward, eight years later, was a U.S.-led regime change that culminated in his violent death. That experience has greatly complicated the task of persuading other states to halt or reverse their nuclear programs. Shortly after the air campaign began, North Korea released a statement from an unnamed Foreign Ministry official saying that "the Libyan crisis is teaching the international community a grave lesson" and that North Korea would not fall for the same U.S. "tactic to disarm the country." Iran's supreme leader, Ayatollah Ali Khamenei, likewise noted that Qaddafi had "wrapped up all his nuclear facilities, packed them on a ship, and delivered them to the West." Another well-connected Iranian, Abbas Abdi, observed: "When Qaddafi was faced with an uprising, all Western leaders dropped him like a brick. Judging from that, our leaders assess that compromise is not helpful."

The intervention in Libya may also have fostered violence in Syria. In March 2011, Syria's uprising was still largely nonviolent, and the Assad government's response, although criminally disproportionate, was relatively circumscribed, claiming the lives of fewer than 100 Syrians per week. After NATO gave Libya's rebels the upper hand, however, Syria's revolutionaries turned to violence in the summer of 2011, perhaps expecting to attract a similar intervention. "It's similar to Benghazi," a Syrian rebel told *The Washington Post* at the time, adding, "We need a no-fly zone." The result was a massive escalation of the Syrian conflict, leading to at least 1,500 deaths per week by early 2013, a 15-fold increase.

NATO's mission in Libya also hindered peacemaking efforts in Syria by greatly antagonizing Russia. With Moscow's acquiescence, the UN Security Council had approved the establishment of a no-fly zone in Libya and other measures to protect civilians. But NATO exceeded that mandate to pursue regime change. The coalition targeted Qaddafi's forces for seven months—even as they retreated, posing no threat to civilians—and armed and trained rebels who rejected peace talks. As Russian President Vladimir Putin complained, NATO forces "frankly violated the UN Security Council resolution on Libya, when instead of imposing the so-called no-fly zone over it they started bombing it too." His foreign minister, Sergey Lavrov, explained that as a result, in Syria, Russia "would never allow the Security Council to authorize anything similar to what happened in Libya."

Early in the Arab Spring, proponents of intervening in Libya had claimed that this course would sustain the momentum of the relatively peaceful uprisings in Tunisia and Egypt. In reality, NATO's action not only failed to spread peaceful revolution but also encouraged the militarization of the uprising in Syria and impeded the prospect of UN intervention there. For Syria and its neighbors, the consequence has been the tragic exacerbation of three pathologies: humanitarian suffering, sectarianism, and radical Islam.

THE ROAD NOT TAKEN

Despite the massive turmoil caused by the intervention, some of its unrepentant supporters claim that the alternative—leaving Qaddafi in power—would have been even worse. But Qaddafi was not Libya's future in any case. Sixty-nine years old and in ill health, he was laying the groundwork for a transition to his son Saif, who for many years had been preparing a reform agenda. "I will not accept any position unless there is a new constitution, new laws, and transparent elections," Saif declared in 2010. "Everyone should have access to public office. We should not have a monopoly on power." Saif also convinced his father that the regime should admit culpability for a notorious 1996 prison massacre and pay compensation to the families of hundreds of victims. In addition, in 2008, Saif published testimony from former prisoners alleging torture by revolutionary committees—the regime's zealous but unofficial watchdogs—whom he demanded be disarmed.

From 2009 to 2010, Saif persuaded his father to release nearly all of Libya's political prisoners, creating a deradicalization program for Islamists that Western experts cited as a model. He also advocated abolishing Libya's Information Ministry in favor of private media. He even flew in renowned American scholars—including Francis Fukuyama, Robert Putnam, and Cass Sunstein—to lecture on civil society and democracy. Perhaps the clearest indication of Saif's reform credentials is that in 2011, the revolution's top political leaders turned out to be officials whom he had brought into the government earlier. Mahmoud Jibril, prime minister of the rebels' National Transitional Council during the war, had led Saif's National Economic Development Board. Mustafa Abdel Jalil, chair of the National Transitional Council, was selected by Saif in 2007 to promote judicial reform as Libya's justice minister, which he did until defecting to the rebels.

Of course, it is impossible to know if Saif would have proved willing or able to transform Libya. He faced opposition from entrenched interests, as even his father did when attempting reform. In 2010, conservatives temporarily closed the media outlets that Saif owned because one of his newspapers had published an op-ed critical of the government. By late 2010, however, the elder Qaddafi had sacked his more hard-line son Mutassim, a move that appeared to pave the way for Saif and his reformist agenda. Although Saif was not going to turn Libya into a Jeffersonian democracy overnight, he did appear intent on eliminating the most egregious inefficiencies and inequities of his father's regime.

Even after the war began, respected observers voiced confidence in Saif. In a *New York Times* op-ed, Curt Weldon, a former ten-term Republican U.S. congressman from Pennsylvania, wrote that Saif "could play a constructive role as a member of the committee to devise a new government structure or Constitution." Instead, NATO-supported militants captured and imprisoned Qaddafi's son. In an October 2014 jailhouse interview with the journalist Franklin Lamb, Saif voiced his regrets: "We were in the process of making broad reforms, and my father gave me the responsibility to see them through. Unfortunately, the revolt happened, and both sides made mistakes that are now allowing extreme Islamist groups like Da'ish [ISIS] to pick up the pieces and turn Libya into an extreme fundamentalist entity."

LEARNING FROM LIBYA

Obama also acknowledges regrets about Libya, but unfortunately, he has drawn the wrong lesson. "I think we underestimated . . . the need to come in full force," the president told the *New York Times* columnist Thomas Friedman in August 2014. "If you're gonna do this," he elaborated, "there has to be a much more aggressive effort to rebuild societies."

But that is exactly the wrong take-away. The error in Libya was not an inadequate post-intervention effort; it was the decision to intervene in the first place. In cases such as Libya, where a government is quashing a rebellion, military intervention is very likely to backfire by fostering violence, state failure, and terrorism. The prospect of intervention also creates perverse incentives for militants to provoke government retaliation and then cry genocide to attract foreign assistance—the moral hazard of humanitarian intervention.

The real lesson of Libya is that when a state is narrowly targeting rebels, the international community needs to refrain from launching a military campaign on humanitarian grounds to help the militants. Western audiences should also beware cynical rebels who exaggerate not only the state's violence but their own popular support, too. Even where a regime is highly flawed, as Qaddafi's was, chances are that intervention will only fuel civil war—destabilizing the country, endangering civilians, and paving the way for extremists. The prudent path is to promote peaceful reform of the type that Qaddafi's son Saif was pursuing.

Humanitarian intervention should be reserved for the rare instances in which civilians are being targeted and military action can do more good than harm, such as Rwanda in 1994, where I have estimated that a timely operation could have saved over 100,000 lives. Of course, great powers sometimes may want to use force abroad for other reasons—to fight terrorism, avert nuclear proliferation, or overthrow a noxious dictator. But they should not pretend the resulting war is humanitarian, or be surprised when it gets a lot of innocent civilians killed.

ISIS Is Not a Terrorist Group

Why Counterterrorism Won't Stop the Latest Jihadist Threat

Audrey Kurth Cronin

On a roll: an ISIS fighter in Raqqa, Syria, June 2014.

After 9/11, many within the U.S. national security establishment worried that, following decades of preparation for confronting conventional enemies, Washington was unready for the challenge posed by an unconventional adversary such as al Qaeda.

AUDREY KURTH CRONIN is Distinguished Professor and Director of the International Security Program at George Mason University and the author of *How Terrorism Ends: Understanding the Decline and Demise of Terrorist Campaigns*. Follow her on Twitter @akcronin.

So over the next decade, the United States built an elaborate bureaucratic structure to fight the jihadist organization, adapting its military and its intelligence and law enforcement agencies to the tasks of counterterrorism and counterinsurgency.

Now, however, a different group, the Islamic State of Iraq and al-Sham (ISIS), which also calls itself the Islamic State, has supplanted al Qaeda as the jihadist threat of greatest concern. ISIS' ideology, rhetoric, and long-term goals are similar to al Qaeda's, and the two groups were once formally allied. So many observers assume that the current challenge is simply to refocus Washington's now-formidable counterterrorism apparatus on a new target.

But ISIS is not al Qaeda. It is not an outgrowth or a part of the older radical Islamist organization, nor does it represent the next phase in its evolution. Although al Qaeda remains dangerous— especially its affiliates in North Africa and Yemen—ISIS is its successor. ISIS represents the post–al Qaeda jihadist threat.

In a nationally televised speech last September explaining his plan to "degrade and ultimately destroy" ISIS, U.S. President Barack Obama drew a straight line between the group and al Qaeda and claimed that ISIS is "a terrorist organization, pure and simple." This was mistaken; ISIS hardly fits that description, and indeed, although it uses terrorism as a tactic, it is not really a terrorist organization at all. Terrorist networks, such as al Qaeda, generally have only dozens or hundreds of members, attack civilians, do not hold territory, and cannot directly confront military forces. ISIS, on the other hand, boasts some 30,000 fighters, holds territory in both Iraq and Syria, maintains extensive military capabilities, controls lines of communication, commands infrastructure, funds itself, and engages in sophisticated military operations. If ISIS is purely and simply anything, it is a pseudo-state led by a conventional army. And that is why the counterterrorism and counterinsurgency strategies that greatly diminished the threat from al Qaeda will not work against ISIS.

Washington has been slow to adapt its policies in Iraq and Syria to the true nature of the threat from ISIS. In Syria, U.S. counterterrorism has mostly prioritized the bombing of al Qaeda affiliates, which has given an edge to ISIS and has also provided the Assad regime with the opportunity to crush U.S.-allied moderate Syrian rebels. In Iraq, Washington continues to rely on a form of counterinsurgency, depending on the central government in Baghdad to regain its lost legitimacy, unite the country, and build indigenous forces to defeat ISIS. These approaches were developed to meet a different threat, and they have been overtaken by events. What's needed now is a strategy of "offensive containment": a combination of limited military tactics and a broad diplomatic strategy to halt ISIS' expansion, isolate the group, and degrade its capabilities.

DIFFERENT STROKES

The differences between al Qaeda and ISIS are partly rooted in their histories. Al Qaeda came into being in the aftermath of the 1979 Soviet invasion of Afghanistan. Its leaders' worldviews and strategic thinking were shaped by the ten-year war against Soviet occupation, when thousands of Muslim militants, including Osama bin Laden, converged on the country. As the organization coalesced, it took the form of a global network focused on carrying out spectacular attacks against Western or Western-allied targets, with the goal of rallying Muslims to join a global confrontation with secular powers near and far.

ISIS came into being thanks to the 2003 U.S. invasion of Iraq. In its earliest incarnation, it was just one of a number of Sunni extremist groups fighting U.S. forces and attacking Shiite civilians in an attempt to foment a sectarian civil war. At that time, it was called al Qaeda in Iraq (AQI), and its leader, Abu Musab al-Zarqawi, had pledged allegiance to bin Laden. Zarqawi was killed by a U.S. air strike in 2006, and soon after, AQI was nearly wiped out when Sunni tribes decided to partner with the Americans to confront the jihadists. But the defeat was temporary; AQI renewed itself inside U.S.-run prisons in Iraq, where insurgents and terrorist operatives connected and formed networks—and where the group's current chief and self-proclaimed caliph, Abu Bakr al-Baghdadi, first distinguished himself as a leader.

In 2011, as a revolt against the Assad regime in Syria expanded into a full-blown civil war, the group took advantage of the chaos, seizing territory in Syria's northeast, establishing a base of operations, and rebranding itself as ISIS. In Iraq, the group continued to capitalize on the weakness of the central state and to exploit the country's sectarian strife, which intensified after U.S. combat forces withdrew. With the Americans gone, Iraqi Prime Minister Nouri al-Maliki pursued a hard-line pro-Shiite agenda, further alienating Sunni Arabs throughout the country. ISIS now counts among its members Iraqi Sunni tribal leaders, former anti-U.S. insurgents, and even secular former Iraqi military officers who seek to regain the power and security they enjoyed during the Saddam Hussein era.

The group's territorial conquest in Iraq came as a shock. When ISIS captured Fallujah and Ramadi in January 2014, most analysts predicted that the U.S.-trained Iraqi security forces would contain the threat. But in June, amid mass desertions from the Iraqi army, ISIS moved toward Baghdad, capturing Mosul, Tikrit, al-Qaim, and numerous other Iraqi towns. By the end of the month, ISIS had renamed itself the Islamic State and had proclaimed the territory under its control to be a new caliphate. Meanwhile, according to U.S. intelligence estimates, some 15,000 foreign fighters from 80 countries flocked to the region to join ISIS, at the rate of around 1,000 per month. Although most of these recruits came from Muslim-majority countries, such as Tunisia and Saudi Arabia, some also hailed from Australia, China, Russia, and western European countries. ISIS has even managed to attract some American teenagers, boys and girls alike, from ordinary middle-class homes in Denver, Minneapolis, and the suburbs of Chicago.

As ISIS has grown, its goals and intentions have become clearer. Al Qaeda conceived of itself as the vanguard of a global insurgency mobilizing Muslim communities against secular rule. ISIS, in contrast, seeks to control territory and create a "pure" Sunni Islamist state governed by a brutal interpretation of sharia; to immediately obliterate the political borders of the Middle East that were created by Western powers in the twentieth century; and to position itself as the sole political, religious, and military authority over all of the world's Muslims.

NOT THE USUAL SUSPECTS

Since ISIS' origins and goals differ markedly from al Qaeda's, the two groups operate in completely different ways. That is why a U.S. counterterrorism strategy custom-made to fight al Qaeda does not fit the struggle against ISIS.

In the post-9/11 era, the United States has built up a trillion-dollar infrastructure of intelligence, law enforcement, and military operations aimed at al Qaeda and its affiliates. According to a 2010 investigation by *The Washington Post*, some 263 U.S. government organizations were created or reorganized in response to the 9/11 attacks, including the Department of Homeland Security, the National Counterterrorism Center, and the Transportation Security Administration. Each year, U.S. intelligence agencies produce some 50,000 reports on terrorism. Fifty-one U.S. federal organizations and military commands track the flow of money to and from terrorist networks. This structure has helped make terrorist attacks on U.S. soil exceedingly rare. In that sense, the system has worked. But it is not well suited for dealing with ISIS, which presents a different sort of challenge.

Consider first the tremendous U.S. military and intelligence campaign to capture or kill al Qaeda's core leadership through drone strikes and Special Forces raids. Some 75 percent of the leaders of the core al Qaeda group have been killed by raids and armed drones, a technology well suited to the task of going after targets hiding in rural areas, where the risk of accidentally killing civilians is lower.

Such tactics, however, don't hold much promise for combating ISIS. The group's fighters and leaders cluster in urban areas, where they are well integrated into civilian populations and usually surrounded by buildings, making drone strikes and raids much harder to carry out. And simply killing ISIS' leaders would not cripple the organization. They govern a functioning pseudo-state with a complex administrative structure. At the top of the military command is the emirate, which consists of Baghdadi and two deputies, both of whom formerly served as generals in the Saddam-era Iraqi army: Abu Ali al-Anbari, who controls ISIS' operations in Syria, and Abu Muslim al-Turkmani, who controls operations in Iraq. ISIS' civilian bureaucracy is supervised by 12 administrators who govern territories in Iraq and Syria, overseeing councils that handle matters such as finances, media, and religious affairs. Although it is hardly the model government depicted in ISIS' propaganda videos, this pseudo-state would carry on quite ably without Baghdadi or his closest lieutenants.

ISIS also poses a daunting challenge to traditional U.S. counterterrorism tactics that take aim at jihadist financing, propaganda, and recruitment. Cutting off al Qaeda's funding has been one of U.S. counterterrorism's most impressive success stories. Soon after the 9/11 attacks, the FBI and the CIA began to coordinate closely on financial intelligence, and they were soon joined by the Department of Defense. FBI agents embedded with U.S. military units during the 2003 invasion of Iraq and debriefed suspected terrorists detained at the U.S. facility at Guantánamo Bay, Cuba. In 2004, the U.S. Treasury Department established the Office of Terrorism and Financial Intelligence, which has cut deeply into al Qaeda's ability to profit from money laundering and receive funds under the cover of charitable giving. A global network for countering terrorist financing has also emerged, backed by the UN, the EU, and hundreds of cooperating governments. The result has been a serious squeeze on al Qaeda's financing; by 2011, the Treasury Department reported that al Qaeda was "struggling to secure steady financing to plan and execute terrorist attacks."

But such tools contribute little to the fight against ISIS, because ISIS does not need outside funding. Holding territory has allowed the group to build a self-sustaining financial model unthinkable for most terrorist groups. Beginning in 2012, ISIS gradually took over key oil assets in eastern Syria; it now controls an estimated 60 percent of the country's oil production capacity. Meanwhile, during its push into Iraq last summer, ISIS also seized seven oil-producing operations in that country. The group manages to sell some of this oil on the black market in Iraq and Syria—including, according to some reports, to the Assad regime itself. ISIS also smuggles oil out of Iraq and Syria into Jordan and Turkey, where it finds plenty of buyers happy to pay below-market prices for illicit crude. All told, ISIS' revenue from oil is estimated to be between $1 million and $3 million per day.

And oil is only one element in the group's financial portfolio. Last June, when ISIS seized control of the northern Iraqi city of Mosul, it looted the provincial central bank and other smaller banks and plundered antiquities to sell on the black market. It steals jewelry, cars, machinery, and livestock from conquered residents. The group also controls major transportation arteries in western Iraq, allowing it to tax the movement of goods and charge tolls. It even earns revenue from cotton and wheat grown in Raqqa, the breadbasket of Syria.

Of course, like terrorist groups, ISIS also takes hostages, demanding tens of millions of dollars in ransom payments. But more important to the group's finances is a wide-ranging extortion racket that targets owners and producers in ISIS territory, taxing everything from small family farms to large enterprises such as cell-phone service providers, water delivery companies, and electric utilities. The enterprise is so complex that the U.S. Treasury has declined to estimate ISIS' total assets and revenues, but ISIS is clearly a highly diversified enterprise whose wealth dwarfs that of any terrorist organization. And there is little evidence that Washington has succeeded in reducing the group's coffers.

SEX AND THE SINGLE JIHADIST

Another aspect of U.S. counterterrorism that has worked well against al Qaeda is the effort to delegitimize the group by publicizing its targeting errors and violent excesses—or by helping U.S. allies do so. Al Qaeda's attacks frequently kill Muslims, and the group's leaders are highly sensitive to the risk this poses to their image as the vanguard of a mass Muslim movement. Attacks in Morocco, Saudi Arabia, and Turkey in 2003; Spain in 2004; and Jordan and the United Kingdom in 2005 all resulted in Muslim casualties that outraged members of Islamic communities everywhere and reduced support for al Qaeda across the Muslim world. The group has steadily lost popular support since around 2007; today, al Qaeda is widely reviled in the Muslim world. The Pew Research Center surveyed nearly 9,000 Muslims in 11 countries in 2013 and found a high median level of disapproval of al Qaeda: 57 percent. In many countries, the number was far higher: 96 percent of Muslims polled in Lebanon, 81 percent in Jordan, 73 percent in Turkey, and 69 percent in Egypt held an unfavorable view of al Qaeda.

ISIS, however, seems impervious to the risk of a backlash. In proclaiming himself the caliph, Baghdadi made a bold (if absurd) claim to religious authority. But ISIS' core message is about raw power and revenge, not legitimacy. Its brutality—videotaped beheadings, mass executions—is designed to intimidate foes and suppress dissent. Revulsion among Muslims at such cruelty might eventually undermine ISIS. But for the time being, Washington's focus on ISIS' savagery only helps the group augment its aura of strength.

For similar reasons, it has proved difficult for the United States and its partners to combat the recruitment efforts that have attracted so many young Muslims to ISIS' ranks. The core al Qaeda group attracted followers with religious arguments and a pseudo-scholarly message of altruism for the sake of the *ummah*, the global Muslim community. Bin Laden and his longtime second-in-command and successor, Ayman al-Zawahiri, carefully constructed an image of religious legitimacy and piety. In their propaganda videos, the men appeared as ascetic warriors, sitting on the ground in caves, studying in libraries, or taking refuge in remote camps. Although some of al Qaeda's affiliates have better recruiting pitches, the core group cast the establishment of a caliphate as a long-term, almost utopian goal: educating and mobilizing the *ummah* came first. In al Qaeda, there is no place for alcohol or women. In this sense, al Qaeda's image is deeply unsexy; indeed, for the young al Qaeda recruit, sex itself comes only after marriage—or martyrdom.

Even for the angriest young Muslim man, this might be a bit of a hard sell. Al Qaeda's leaders' attempts to depict themselves as moral—even moralistic—figures have limited their appeal. Successful deradicalization programs in places such as Indonesia and Singapore have zeroed in on the mismatch between what al Qaeda offers and what most young people are really interested in, encouraging militants to reintegrate into society, where their more prosaic hopes and desires might be fulfilled more readily.

ISIS, in contrast, offers a very different message for young men, and sometimes women. The group attracts followers yearning for not only religious righteousness but also adventure, personal power, and a sense of self and community. And, of course, some people just want to kill—and ISIS welcomes them, too. The group's brutal violence attracts attention, demonstrates dominance, and draws people to the action.

ISIS operates in urban settings and offers recruits immediate opportunities to fight. It advertises by distributing exhilarating podcasts produced by individual fighters on the frontlines. The group also procures sexual partners for its male recruits; some of these women volunteer for this role, but most of them are coerced or even enslaved. The group barely bothers to justify this behavior in religious terms; its sales pitch is conquest in all its forms, including the sexual kind. And it has already established a self-styled caliphate, with Baghdadi as the caliph, thus making present (if only in a limited way, for now) what al Qaeda generally held out as something more akin to a utopian future.

In short, ISIS offers short-term, primitive gratification. It does not radicalize people in ways that can be countered by appeals to logic. Teenagers are attracted to the group without even understanding what it is, and older fighters just want to be associated with ISIS' success. Compared with fighting al Qaeda's relatively austere message, Washington has found it much harder to counter ISIS' more visceral appeal, perhaps for a very simple reason: a desire for power, agency, and instant results also pervades American culture.

2015 ≠ 2006

Counterterrorism wasn't the only element of national security practice that Washington rediscovered and reinvigorated after 9/11; counterinsurgency also enjoyed a renaissance. As chaos erupted in Iraq in the aftermath of the U.S. invasion and occupation of 2003, the U.S. military grudgingly starting thinking about counterinsurgency, a subject that had fallen out of favor in the national security establishment after the Vietnam War. The most successful application of U.S. counterinsurgency doctrine was the 2007 "surge" in Iraq, overseen by General David Petraeus. In 2006, as violence peaked in Sunni-dominated Anbar Province, U.S. officials concluded that the United States was losing the war. In response, President George W. Bush decided to send an additional 20,000 U.S. troops to Iraq. General John Allen, then serving as deputy commander of the multinational forces in Anbar, cultivated relationships with local Sunni tribes and nurtured the so-called Sunni Awakening, in which some 40 Sunni tribes or subtribes essentially switched sides and decided to fight with the newly augmented U.S. forces against AQI. By the summer of 2008, the number of insurgent attacks had fallen by more than 80 percent.

Looking at the extent of ISIS' recent gains in Sunni areas of Iraq, which have undone much of the progress made in the surge, some have argued that Washington should respond with a second application of the Iraq war's counterinsurgency strategy. And the White House seems at least partly persuaded by this line of thinking: last year, Obama asked Allen to act as a special envoy for building an anti-ISIS coalition in the region. There is a certain logic to this approach, since ISIS draws support from many of the same insurgent groups that the surge and the Sunni Awakening neutralized— groups that have reemerged as threats thanks to the vacuum created by the withdrawal of U.S. forces in 2011 and Maliki's sectarian rule in Baghdad.

But vast differences exist between the situation today and the one that Washington faced in 2006, and the logic of U.S. counterinsurgency does not suit the struggle against ISIS. The United States cannot win the hearts and minds of Iraq's Sunni Arabs, because the Maliki government has already lost them. The Shiite-dominated Iraqi government has so badly undercut its own political legitimacy that it might be impossible to restore it. Moreover, the United States no longer occupies Iraq. Washington can send in more troops, but it cannot lend legitimacy to a government it no longer controls. ISIS is less an insurgent group fighting against an established government than one party in a conventional civil war between a breakaway territory and a weak central state.

DIVIDE AND CONQUER?

The United States has relied on counterinsurgency strategy not only to reverse Iraq's slide into state failure but also to serve as a model for how to combat the wider jihadist movement. Al Qaeda expanded by persuading Muslim militant groups all over the world to turn their more narrowly targeted nationalist campaigns into nodes in al Qaeda's global jihad—and, sometimes, to convert themselves into al Qaeda affiliates. But there was little commonality in the visions pursued by Chechen, Filipino, Indonesian, Kashmiri, Palestinian, and Uighur militants, all of whom bin Laden tried to draw into al Qaeda's tent, and al Qaeda often had trouble fully reconciling its own goals with the interests of its far-flung affiliates.

That created a vulnerability, and the United States and its allies sought to exploit it. Governments in Indonesia and the Philippines won dramatic victories against al Qaeda affiliates in their countries by combining counterterrorism operations with relationship building in local communities, instituting deradicalization programs, providing religious training in prisons, using rehabilitated former terrorist operatives as government spokespeople, and sometimes negotiating over local grievances.

Some observers have called for Washington to apply the same strategy to ISIS by attempting to expose the fault lines between the group's secular former Iraqi army officers, Sunni tribal leaders, and Sunni resistance fighters, on the one hand, and its veteran jihadists, on the other. But it's too late for that approach to work. ISIS is now led by well-trained, capable former Iraqi military leaders who know U.S. techniques and habits because Washington helped train them. And after routing Iraqi army units and taking their U.S.-supplied equipment, ISIS is now armed with American tanks, artillery, armored Humvees, and mine-resistant vehicles.

Perhaps ISIS' harsh religious fanaticism will eventually prove too much for their secular former Baathist allies. But for now, the Saddam-era officers are far from reluctant warriors for ISIS: rather, they are leading the charge. In their hands, ISIS has developed a sophisticated light-infantry army, brandishing American weapons.

Of course, this opens up a third possible approach to ISIS, besides counterterrorism and counterinsurgency: a full-on conventional war against the group, waged with the goal of completely destroying it. Such a war would be folly. After experiencing more than a decade of continuous war, the American public simply would not support the long-term occupation and intense fighting that would be required to obliterate ISIS. The pursuit of a full-fledged military campaign would exhaust U.S. resources and offer little hope of obtaining the objective. Wars pursued at odds with political reality cannot be won.

CONTAINING THE THREAT

The sobering fact is that the United States has no good military options in its fight against ISIS. Neither counterterrorism, nor counterinsurgency, nor conventional warfare is likely to afford Washington a clear-cut victory against the group. For the time being, at least, the policy that best matches ends and means and that has the best chance of securing U.S. interests is one of offensive containment: combining a limited military campaign with a major diplomatic and economic effort to weaken ISIS and align the interests of the many countries that are threatened by the group's advance.

ISIS is not merely an American problem. The wars in Iraq and Syria involve not only regional players but also major global actors, such as Russia, Turkey, Iran, Saudi Arabia, and other Gulf states. Washington must stop behaving as if it can fix the region's problems with military force and instead resurrect its role as a diplomatic superpower.

Of course, U.S. military force would be an important part of an offensive containment policy. Air strikes can pin ISIS down, and cutting off its supply of technology, weapons, and ammunition by choking off smuggling routes would further weaken the group. Meanwhile, the United States should continue to advise and support the Iraqi military, assist regional forces such as the Kurdish Pesh Merga, and provide humanitarian assistance to civilians fleeing ISIS' territory. Washington should also expand its assistance to neighboring countries such as Jordan and Lebanon, which are struggling to contend with the massive flow of refugees from Syria. But putting more U.S. troops on the ground would be counterproductive, entangling the United States in an unwinnable war that could go on for decades. The United States cannot rebuild the Iraqi state or determine the outcome of the Syrian civil war. Frustrating as it might be to some, when it comes to military action, Washington should stick to a realistic course that recognizes the limitations of U.S. military force as a long-term solution.

The Obama administration's recently convened "summit on countering violent extremism"—which brought world leaders to Washington to discuss how to combat radical jihadism—was a valuable exercise. But although it highlighted the existing threat posed by al Qaeda's regional affiliates, it also reinforced the idea that ISIS is primarily a counterterrorism challenge. In fact, ISIS poses a much greater risk: it seeks to challenge the current international order, and, unlike the greatly diminished core al Qaeda organization, it is coming closer to actually achieving that goal. The United States cannot single-handedly defend the region and the world from an aggressive revisionist theocratic state—nor should it. The major powers must develop a common diplomatic, economic, and military approach to ensure that this pseudo-state is tightly contained and treated as a global pariah. The good news is that no government supports ISIS; the group has managed to make itself an enemy of every state in the region—and, indeed, the world. To exploit that fact, Washington should pursue a more aggressive, top-level diplomatic agenda with major powers and regional players, including Iran, Saudi Arabia, France, Germany, the United Kingdom, Russia, and even China, as well as Iraq's and Syria's neighbors, to design a unified response to ISIS.

That response must go beyond making a mutual commitment to prevent the radicalization and recruitment of would-be jihadists and beyond the regional military coalition that the United States has built. The major powers and regional players must agree to stiffen the international arms embargo currently imposed on ISIS, enact more vigorous sanctions against the group, conduct joint border patrols, provide more aid for displaced persons and refugees, and strengthen UN peacekeeping missions in countries that border Iraq and Syria. Although some of these tools overlap with counterterrorism, they should be put in the service of a strategy for fighting an enemy more akin to a state actor: ISIS is not a nuclear power, but the group represents a threat to international stability equivalent to that posed by North Korea. It should be treated no less seriously.

Given that political posturing over U.S. foreign policy will only intensify as the 2016 U.S. presidential election approaches, the White House would likely face numerous attacks on a containment approach that would satisfy neither the hawkish nor the anti-interventionist camp within the U.S. national security establishment. In the face of such criticism, the United States must stay committed to fighting ISIS over the long term in a manner that matches ends with means, calibrating and improving U.S. efforts to contain the group by moving past outmoded forms of counterterrorism and counterinsurgency while also resisting pressure to cross the threshold into full-fledged war. Over time, the successful containment of ISIS might open up better policy options. But for the foreseeable future, containment is the best policy that the United States can pursue.

The End of Reform in China

Authoritarian Adaptation Hits a Wall

Youwei

MARK RALSTON / AFP / GETTY IMAGES

Mad in China: a labor protest in Beijing, January 2013

Since the start of its post-Mao reforms in the late 1970s, the communist regime in China has repeatedly defied predictions of its impending demise. The key to its success lies in what one might call "authoritarian adaptation"—the use of policy reforms to substitute for fundamental institutional change. Under Deng Xiaoping, this meant reforming agriculture and unleashing

YOUWEI is a pseudonym for a scholar based in China.

entrepreneurship. Under Jiang Zemin, it meant officially enshrining a market economy, reforming state-owned enterprises, and joining the World Trade Organization. Under Hu Jintao and Wen Jiabao, it meant reforming social security. Many expect yet another round of sweeping reforms under Xi Jinping—but they may be disappointed.

The need for further reforms still exists, due to widespread corruption, rising inequality, slowing growth, and environmental problems. But the era of authoritarian adaptation is reaching its end, because there is not much potential for further evolution within China's current authoritarian framework. A self-strengthening equilibrium of stagnation is being formed, which will be hard to break without some major economic, social, or international shock.

IS CHINA EXCEPTIONAL?

One reason for the loss of steam is that most easy reforms have already been launched. Revamping agriculture, encouraging entrepreneurship, promoting trade, tweaking social security—all these have created new benefits and beneficiaries while imposing few costs on established interests. What is left are the harder changes, such as removing state monopolies in critical sectors of the economy, privatizing land, giving the National People's Congress power over fiscal issues, and establishing an independent court system. Moving forward with these could begin to threaten the hold of the Chinese Communist Party on power, something that the regime is unwilling to tolerate.

Another reason for the loss of steam is the formation of an increasingly strong antireform bloc. Few want to reverse the reforms that have already taken place, since these have grown the pie dramatically. But many in the bureaucracy and the elite more generally would be happy with the perpetuation of the status quo, because partial reform is the best friend of crony capitalism.

What about society at large? Modernization theory predicts that economic development empowers society, which eventually leads to political transformation. With a per capita GDP of roughly $7,000, is China succumbing to this logic? Many argue that the country will not, because it is exceptional. Political legitimacy in China rests more on the goods government provides than the rights it protects, they claim. Entrepreneurs are co-opted, students are distracted by nationalism, peasants and workers are interested only in material justice. More likely, however, what is exceptional in China is not society or culture but the state.

In China, as elsewhere, economic development has led to contention: peasants are demanding lower taxes, workers want more labor protections, students are forming activist groups, entrepreneurs are starting charities, media organizations have begun muckraking, and lawyers are defending human rights. Collective action has soared, and the country now has more than a million grass-roots nongovernmental organizations. And the Internet poses a big challenge for the regime, by linking ordinary people to one another—and to intellectuals.

However, it takes organizational skills and ideological articulation for practical pursuits to mature into political demands. These

REUTERS / STRINGER

An protest against the government's plans to construct a petrochemical plant in Zhejiang province, October 2012.

require at least some political space to develop, and such space is almost nonexistent in China. If the Chinese Communist Party has learned anything from the 1989 democracy movement and the Soviet experience, it is the lesson that "a single spark can start a prairie fire," as the Chinese saying goes. Equipped with tremendous resources, the regime gradually developed an omnipresent, sophisticated, and extremely efficient apparatus of "stability maintenance," which has successfully prevented the second half of modernization theory's logic from being realized. This system for ensuring domestic security is designed to nip any sign of opposition, real or imagined, in the bud. Prevention is even more important than repression—in fact, violent suppression of protests is seen as a sign of failure. China's strong state is reflected not so much in its sharp teeth as in its nimble fingers.

Speech is censored, in the press and on the Internet, to prevent the publication of anything deemed "troublesome." Actions are watched even more closely. Even seemingly nonpolitical actions can be considered dangerous; in 2014, Xu Zhiyong, a legal activist who had led a campaign for equal educational opportunities for the children of rural migrants, was sentenced to four years in prison for "disturbing public order." Public gatherings are restricted, and even private gatherings can be problematic. In May 2014, several scholars and lawyers were detained after attending a memorial meeting for the 1989 movement in a private home. Even the signing of petitions can bring retribution.

Just as important is the emerging mass line—that is, official public guidance—about China's critical need to maintain stability. A grid of security management has been put in place across the entire country, including extensive security bureaucracies and an extra-bureaucratic network of patrol forces, traffic assistants, and population monitors. Hundreds of thousands of "security volunteers," or "security informants," have been recruited among taxi drivers, sanitation workers, parking-lot attendants, and street peddlers to report on "suspicious people or activity." One Beijing neighborhood reportedly boasts 2,400 "building unit leaders" who

REUTERS / DAVID GRAY

Paramilitary policemen at Tiananmen Square, November 2012.

can note any irregularity in minutes, with the going rate for pieces of information set at two yuan (about 30 cents). This system tracks criminal and terrorist threats along with political troublemakers, but dissenters are certainly among its prime targets.

In today's China, Big Brother is everywhere. The domestic security net is as strong yet as delicate as a spider web, as omnipresent yet as shapeless as water. People smart enough to avoid politics entirely will not even feel it. Should they cross the line, however, the authorities of this shadow world would snap into action quickly. Official overreaction is a virtue, not a vice: "chopping a chicken using the blade for a cow," as the saying goes, is fully approved, the better to prevent trouble from getting out of hand.

This system is good at maintaining order. But it has reduced the chances of any mature civil society developing in contemporary China, let alone a political one. And so even as grievances proliferate, the balance of power between the state and society leans overwhelmingly toward the former. Social movements, like plants, need space in which to grow. And when such space does not exist, both movements and plants wither.

THE BURIED GIANT

Lacking support from above or below, reform in China has now stagnated, and may even be moving backward. The current leadership still embraces the rhetoric of reform, and it has indeed launched some reform initiatives. Yet they tend to be, as the Chinese say, "loud thunder, small raindrops."

The most significant is Xi's anticorruption campaign. Having brought about the downfall of 74 provincial-level officials over the past two-plus years, in addition to hundreds of thousands of lower officials, the campaign is certainly vigorous. In the three decades before Xi took power, only three national officials lost their positions for corruption; in less than three years under Xi, five have already done so. Yet the anticorruption campaign should not really be considered a reform program. Instead of encouraging freer media, more independent courts, and watchdog groups to expose and check corruption, the campaign is driven and controlled from the top and characterized by secrecy, ruthlessness, and political calculation. Yu Qiyi, an engineer at a state-owned enterprise who was accused of corruption, died of torture while being interrogated in 2013. Zhou Wenbin, a former president of Nanchang University, has also claimed to have been tortured, in early 2015. This is reminiscent of the Maoist "rectification" campaigns (albeit much less intense) or even disciplinary actions in imperial China. Such campaigns tend to produce more concentration of power rather than less, strengthening the legitimacy of particular charismatic leaders at the expense of bureaucracies.

Small reforms are moving forward in some other areas as well, but none of them is transformational. The 18th Party Congress, held in late 2012, emphasized judiciary reform, but so far, nothing much more than administrative restructuring has happened. A Central Committee edict in late 2014 promised to strengthen "institutions of independent and fair trials and prosecution," but it set the first principle of legal reform as "asserting the leadership of the

Chinese Communist Party." Party officials frequently nod to the importance of "deliberative democracy," and early this year, the party released a plan to "strengthen socialist deliberative democracy," but it is unclear how deliberation can be made meaningful without ways of punishing institutional unresponsiveness.

There has also been repeated talk about reforming the laws and rules that apply to nongovernmental organizations. Progress in this area, however, is slow and dubious, as demonstrated by the forced dissolution of the Liren Rural Library project, which was focused on extracurricular learning in rural China. The economic arena has seen some genuine reforms, such as the reduction of licensing barriers for businesses and the introduction of more competition in banking, but many see the efforts as mild, with state monopolies in several areas largely untouched. And in social policy, the loosening up of the national one-child policy represents progress, but it may not be enough to make much of a difference.

Underlying the inertia is ideological deadlock. The so-called socialist market economy principle has guided China for over 30 years, allowing for both continuity and reform. It has always contained something of an internal contradiction, because the impersonal legal system required by the market economy could potentially compete with the personalized party leadership as the final arbiter of public affairs, and in recent years, the question has come to the fore with greater urgency: Which is more important, the needs of the market economy or those of the Communist Party?

In practice, the needs of the party prevail. But the regime has not developed a coherent, contemporary ideological discourse to justify that outcome. Marxism is obviously inadequate. The regime increasingly resorts to Confucianism, with its convenient emphasis on benevolent governance within a hierarchical order. Yet the two coexist uneasily because the party still nominally embraces Marxism-Leninism, whose emphasis on equality goes against Confucianism, which stresses hierarchy.

What Xi presents most often are the so-called socialist core values. Now posted everywhere in China, these include "prosperity,

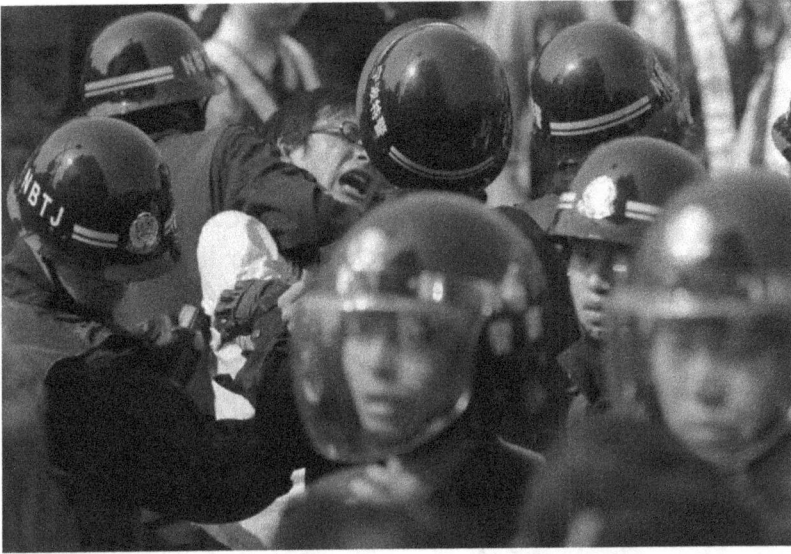

REUTERS / CARLOS BARRIA

A protester getting detained in Zhejiang province, October 2012.

democracy, civility, harmony, freedom, equality, justice, the rule of law, patriotism, dedication, integrity, friendship." The list reads more like an ad hoc patchwork than a coherent vision. It reflects anxiety more than confidence, and with good reason: a praxis without ideological grounding is weak and unsustainable.

FOUR FUTURES

China faces four possible futures. In the first, which the party favors, the country would become a "Singapore on steroids," as the China expert Elizabeth Economy has written. If the anticorruption campaign is thorough and sustainable, a new party might be born, one that could govern China with efficiency and benevolence. Policy reforms would continue, the country's economic potential would be unleashed, and the resulting productivity and progress would boost the new party's legitimacy and power.

Such a future is unlikely, however, for many reasons. For one thing, Singapore is much less authoritarian than contemporary China; it has multiple parties and much more political freedom.

Political competition is not completely fair, but opposition parties won 40 percent of the popular vote in elections in 2011. For China to emulate Singapore, it would have to open up political competition significantly, possibly stepping onto a slippery slope to full pluralistic democracy—an outcome the Communist Party does not want to risk. Singapore is tiny, moreover, and so the cost of supervising its administration is relatively small. China is huge, and the party would find it increasingly difficult to supervise the country's vast, multilevel governmental apparatus from the top down.

The second and most likely future, at least in the short term, is a continuation of the status quo. Whatever problems it has, the regime's current model of "socialism with Chinese characteristics" is not exhausted. From demographics to urbanization to globalization to the revolution in information technology, the structural factors that have facilitated China's rise are still present and will continue to operate for some years to come, and the regime can continue to benefit from them.

But not forever: a regime relying on performance legitimacy needs continued economic growth to maintain itself in power. With growth already slowing, fear of a hard landing is rising. A housing bubble, manufacturing overcapacity, financial instability, weak domestic demand, and widening inequality represent significant vulnerabilities. The bursting of the housing bubble, for example, could cause problems throughout the economy and then in the political sector, too, as local governments lost a major fiscal source that they rely on to support public services and domestic security.

This could trigger the third possible future: democratization through a crisis. Such an outcome would not be pretty. With the country's economy damaged and political demands soaring, conflicts could intensify rather than subside, and several time bombs planted by the current regime (a demographic crisis, environmental devastation, ethnic tensions) could eventually explode, making matters worse. The result might be the reemergence of some form of authoritarianism as the country recoiled from democratic disorder.

A fourth scenario—controlled and sequenced democratization—would be the best for China but is unfortunately unlikely. An enlightened leadership in Beijing could take steps now to lay the groundwork for an eventual transition, with multiparty elections organized as the final step of the process, well down the road. Enabling gradual judicial independence, empowering the National People's Congress to deal with fiscal issues, encouraging the development of civil society, and introducing intraparty competition are measures that could pave the way for a smoother transition later on, and that in conjunction with reforms on policies relating to population control, minorities, and the environment could help China dodge some future trauma. Such prepared and sequenced reform, however, would require a coalition of pro-reform politicians within the leadership, which is absent now and unlikely to appear soon.

As for outsiders, what they can do is limited. External pressure tends to ignite defensive nationalism rather than indigenous liberalism. For a country with China's size and history, democratization will have to emerge from within. But the fact that the world's most powerful countries tend to be liberal democracies creates a strong ideological pull—and so the best way for the West to help China's eventual political evolution is to remain strong, liberal, democratic, and successful itself.

The Decline of International Studies

Why Flying Blind Is Dangerous

Charles King

Princeton's Woodrow Wilson School of Public and International Affairs, April 1989.

I n October 2013, the U.S. Department of State eliminated its funding program for advanced language and cultural training on Russia and the former Soviet Union. Created in 1983 as a

CHARLES KING is Professor of International Affairs and Chair of the Department of Government at Georgetown University. His most recent book is Midnight at the Pera Palace: The Birth of Modern Istanbul. Follow him on Twitter @charleskingdc.

special appropriation by Congress, the so-called Title VIII Program had supported generations of specialists working in academia, think tanks, and the U.S. government itself. But as a State Department official told the Russian news service RIA Novosti at the time, "In this fiscal climate, it just didn't make it." The program's shuttering came just a month before the start of a now well-known chain of events: Ukraine's Euromaidan revolution, Russia's annexation of Crimea, and the descent of U.S.-Russian relations to their lowest level since the Cold War. The timing was, to say the least, unfortunate.

The end of the United States' premier federal program for Russian studies saved taxpayers only $3.3 million—the cost of two Tomahawk cruise missiles or about half a day's sea time for an aircraft carrier strike group. The development was part of a broader trend: the scaling back of a long-term national commitment to education and research focused on international affairs. Two years ago, the American Academy of Arts and Sciences warned of a hidden crisis in the humanities and social sciences. "Now more than ever," the academy's report concluded, "the spirit of international cooperation, the promotion of trade and foreign investment, the requirements of international diplomacy, and even the enhancement of national security depend in some measure on an American citizenry trained in humanistic and social scientific disciplines, including languages, transnational studies, moral and political philosophy, global ethics, and international relations." In response to lobbying by universities and scholarly associations, Title VIII was resuscitated earlier this year, but it came back at less than half its previous funding level and with future appropriations left uncertain. Given the mounting challenges that Washington faces in Russia and eastern Europe, now seems to be an especially odd time to reduce federal support for educating the next cohort of experts.

The rise of the United States as a global power was the product of more than merely economic and military advantages. Where the country was truly hegemonic was in its unmatched knowledge of the hidden interior of other nations: their languages and cultures, their histories and political systems, their local economies and human geographies. Through programs such as Title VIII, the U.S. government created a remarkable community of minutemen of the mind: scholars, graduate students, and undergraduates who possessed the linguistic skills, historical sensitivity, and sheer intellectual curiosity to peer deeply into foreign societies. Policymakers sometimes learned to listen to them, and not infrequently, these scholars even became policymakers themselves.

That knowledge flourished in an environment defined by some of the great innovations of American higher education: unfettered inquiry, the assessment of scholarship via rigorous peer review, the expectation that the value of discovery lies somewhere other than in its immediate usefulness, and the link between original research and innovative teaching. If you want evidence-based expertise on terrorism in Pakistan, environmental degradation in China, or local politics in provincial Russia, there is someone in an American university who can provide it. It is harder to imagine a Pakistani scholar who knows Nebraska, a Chinese researcher who can speak with authority about the revival of Detroit, or a Russian professor who wields original survey data on the next U.S. presidential race.

But things are changing. Shifting priorities at the national level, a misreading of the effects of globalization, and academics' own drift away from knowing real things about real places have combined to weaken this vital component of the United States' intellectual capital. Educational institutions and the disciplines they preserve are retreating from the task of cultivating men and women who are comfortable moving around the globe, both literally and figuratively. Government agencies, in turn, are reducing their overall support and narrowing it to fields deemed relevant to U.S. national security—and even to specific research topics within them. Worse, academic research is now subject to the same "culture war" attacks that federal lawmakers used to reserve for profane rap lyrics and blasphemous artwork. Unless Washington stops this downward spiral, these changes will not only weaken national readiness. They will also erode the habit of mind that good international affairs

GERALD R. FORD SCHOOL OF PUBLIC POLICY / FLICKR

University of Michigan students videoconference with the USAID director for Mexico, August 2014.

education was always supposed to produce: an appreciation for people, practices, and ideas that are not one's own.

LOST IN TRANSLATION?

Americans naturally swing between isolation and engagement with the world, but it is government that has usually nudged them in one direction or the other. A century ago, rates of foreign-language study in Europe and the United States were about the same, with roughly a third of secondary school students in both places learning a modern foreign language. After the United States entered World War I, however, almost half the U.S. states criminalized the teaching of German or other foreign languages in schools. It took a Supreme Court decision in 1923 to overturn that practice.

During World War II, the U.S. government made attempts to train up linguists and instant area experts, but these initiatives quickly faded. It was not until the onset of the Cold War that private universities such as Columbia and Harvard devoted serious attention to the problem and opened pioneering programs for

Russian studies. The Carnegie, Ford, and Rockefeller Foundations launched grants for scholars working specifically on Soviet politics, history, or economics.

Only in the late 1950s did the focus on what is now known as internationalization become a national priority—a response to the Sputnik scare and the sense that the Soviets could soon gain superiority in fields well beyond science and technology. The National Defense Education Act of 1958, followed by the Higher Education Act of 1965 and its successors, provided special funding for regional studies and advanced language training for American graduate students. Among other measures, the legislation created a network of National Resource Centers located at major U.S. universities, which in turn ran master's programs and other forms of instruction to train the next generation of specialists. In 2010, the total size of this allocation, known as Title VI, stood at $110 million, distributed across programs for East Asia, Latin America, the Middle East, Russia and Eurasia, and other areas. Along with the Fulbright-Hays scholarships for international academic exchanges, established in 1961, Title VI became one of the principal sources of funding for future political scientists, historians, linguists, anthropologists, and others working on distinct world regions.

On the face of it, that investment seems to have paid off. American universities have emerged as among the world's most globally minded. No U.S. college president can long survive without developing a strategy for further internationalization. New schools for specialized study have sprung up across the United States—for example, the University of Oklahoma's College of International Studies, founded in 2011, and Indiana University's School of Global and International Studies, which opened in 2012. Older centers—including Georgetown University's Edmund A. Walsh School of Foreign Service, Johns Hopkins University's School of Advanced International Studies, Princeton University's Woodrow Wilson School of Public and International Affairs, Tufts University's Fletcher School of Law and Diplomacy, and George Washington University's Elliott School of International Affairs—consistently top world rankings. The U.S. example has become the model for a raft of new institutions around the world, such as the Hertie School of Governance in Berlin and the Lee Kuan Yew School of Public Policy in Singapore, founded in 2003 and 2004, respectively, and the Blavatnik School of Government at Oxford University, founded in 2010.

True, young Americans can play video games with their peers in Cairo, chat online with friends in St. Petersburg, and download music from a punk band based in Beijing. But consuming the world is not the same as understanding it. After a steady expansion over two decades, enrollment in foreign-language courses at U.S. colleges fell by 6.7 percent between 2009 and 2013. Most language programs experienced double-digit losses. Even Spanish—a language chosen by more U.S. students than all other languages combined—has suffered its first decline since the Modern Language Association began keeping count in 1958. Today, the third most studied language in U.S. higher education, behind Spanish and French, is a homegrown one: American Sign Language.

Something similar has happened in the unlikeliest of places: among professional scholars of international relations. According to an annual survey conducted by the College of William and Mary, 30 percent of American researchers in the field say that they have a working knowledge of no language other than English, and more than half say that they rarely or never cite non-English sources in their work. (Forty percent, however, rank Chinese as the most valuable language for their students to know after English.) At least within the United States, the remarkable growth in the study of international relations in recent decades has produced one of the academy's more parochial disciplines.

Part of the problem lies in the professoriate. An iron law of academia holds that, with time, all disciplines bore even themselves. English professors drift away from novels and toward literary theory. Economists envy mathematicians. Political scientists give up grappling with dilemmas of power and governance—the concerns of thinkers from Aristotle to Max Weber and Hans Morgenthau—and make their own pastiche of the natural sciences with careful hypotheses about minute problems. Being monumentally wrong is less attractive than being unimportantly right. Research questions derive almost exclusively from what has gone unsaid in some previous scholarly conversation. As any graduate student learns early on, one must first "fill a hole in the literature" and only later figure out whether it was worth filling. Doctoral programs also do a criminally poor job of teaching young scholars to write and speak in multiple registers—that is, use jargon with their peers if necessary but then explain their findings to a broader audience with equal zeal and effectiveness.

Still, the cultishness of the American academy can be overstated. Today, younger scholars of Russia and Eurasia, for example, have language skills and local knowledge that are the envy of their older colleagues—in part because of decades of substantial federal investment in the field and in part because many current students actually hail from the region and have chosen to make their careers in American universities. Even the increasing quantification of political science can be a boon when abstract concepts are combined with

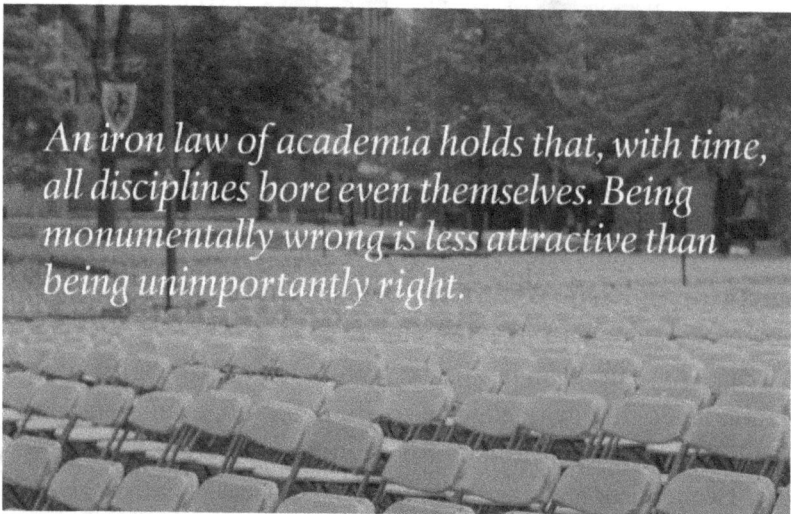

An iron law of academia holds that, with time, all disciplines bore even themselves. Being monumentally wrong is less attractive than being unimportantly right.

TIM SACKTON / FLICKR

A sea of chairs ahead of Harvard University's 2013 commencement.

grass-roots understanding of specific contexts. Statistical modeling, field experiments, and "big data" have revolutionized areas as diverse as development economics, public health, and product marketing. There is no reason that similar techniques shouldn't enrich the study of international affairs, and the private sector is already forging ahead in that area. Companies such as Dataminr—a start-up that analyzes social-media postings for patterns to detect breaking news—now track everything from environmental crises to armed conflict. Foreign policy experts used to debate the causes of war. Now they can see them unspooling in real time.

The deeper problems are matters of money and partisan politics. In an Internet-connected world infused with global English, private funders have radically scaled back their support for work that requires what the political scientist Richard Fenno called "soaking and poking": studying difficult languages, living in unfamiliar communities, and making sense of complex histories and cultures. Very few of the major U.S. foundations finance international and regional studies on levels approaching those of two decades ago. Foundation boards, influenced by the modish language of disruption and social entrepreneurship, want projects with actionable ideas and measurable impact. Over the short term, serious investments in building hard-to-acquire skills are unlikely to yield either. And these developments don't represent a mere shift from the study of Russia and Eurasia to a focus on the Middle East and East Asia—a pivot that would be reasonable given changes in global politics. The Carnegie Corporation of New York, for example, ended its prestigious senior fellowship program on Muslim societies in 2009 and wound down its wider Islam Initiative shortly thereafter.

The U.S. government has followed suit. The suspension of Title VIII was only the latest in a series of cutbacks. The Foreign Language Assistance Program, created in 1988 to provide local schools with matching grants from the Department of Education for teaching foreign languages, ended in 2012. The previous year, Title VI funding for university-based regional studies fell by 40 percent and has flatlined since. If today's Title VI appropriation were

BRIAN SNYDER / REUTERS

Students take their seats for the diploma ceremony at the John F. Kennedy School of Government during the 361st Commencement Exercises at Harvard University in Cambridge, Massachusetts May 24, 2012.

funded at the level it was during the Johnson administration, then it would total almost half a billion dollars after adjusting for inflation. Instead, the 2014 number stood at slightly below $64 million.

The same thing has happened with direct funding to undergraduates and graduate students, particularly when it comes to the National Security Education Program (NSEP), which offers students financial assistance for foreign-language study and cultural immersion. NSEP was established in 1991 on the initiative of David Boren, then a Democratic senator from Oklahoma, with the goal of training a new, post–Cold War generation of foreign affairs specialists. The program's signature elements—Boren Scholarships and Boren Fellowships—offer grants of up to $30,000 to highly qualified undergraduates and graduate students in exchange for at least a year of federal government service in national security after graduation. For all its prestige, however, and despite nominal support among both liberals and conservatives, the Boren program offers fewer such awards today than it did in the mid-1990s.

Another element of NSEP is an innovative initiative for heritage speakers—American citizens who possess native abilities in a foreign language and wish to develop professional-level skills in English—and it, too, has shrunk. The initiative has never been able to fund more than 40 people per year, most of them native speakers of Arabic or Mandarin, and the number has been steadily falling, reaching just 18 in 2014. (This program is now housed at Georgetown University, where I teach.) In a somewhat encouraging sign, enrollment has been growing markedly in NSEP's Language Flagship program, which gives grants to colleges to field advanced courses in languages deemed important for national security. But the raw numbers reveal just how small the United States' next generation of linguists actually is. Last year, the total number of students enrolled in NSEP-sponsored courses for all the "critical languages"—Arabic, Chinese, Hindi, Korean, Persian, Portuguese, Russian, Swahili, Turkish, Urdu, and Yoruba—was under a thousand.

In tandem with these trends, scholarly research in global affairs, especially work funded by the National Science Foundation, has come under growing attack. The annual appropriation for the NSF is around $7.3 billion, of which a fraction—less than $260 million—goes to the behavioral, social, and economic sciences. Of that figure, only about $13 million goes to political scientists, and an even smaller amount goes to those doing research on international affairs. Still, these scholars now receive the kind of lambasting that used to be directed mainly against the National Endowment for the Arts.

As just one example, for the past two years, the NSF has been the particular focus of the House Committee on Science, Space, and Technology, which oversees the foundation along with portions of the Federal Aviation Administration, NASA, and other agencies. The committee intends to subject all NSF-funded projects to a relevance test that would require the foundation to certify that every taxpayer dollar is spent "in the national interest." In a recent opinion piece for *The Hill*, Lamar Smith, the Republican representative from Texas who chairs the committee, pilloried NSF-funded researchers working on the environmental history of New Zealand, women and Islam in Turkey, and local politics in India. "How about studying the United States of America?" he wrote. "Federal research agencies have an obligation to explain to American taxpayers why their money is being used to provide free foreign vacations to college professors." In response to this kind of criticism, academic associations have hired their own lobbyists—a recognition of the fact that education and research are now less national priorities than objects of political jockeying, on par with items on the wish lists of private corporations and interest groups.

The crusade for relevance is part of a broader development: the growing militarization of government-funded scholarship. Researchers in international and regional studies have always doffed a hat to strategic priorities. Even historians and literature professors became accustomed to touting their work's policy significance when they applied for federal grants and fellowships. But today, a substantial portion of assistance comes directly from the U.S. Department of Defense. The department's Minerva Initiative provides support for research on "areas of strategic importance to U.S. national security policy" and for "projects addressing specific topic areas determined by the Secretary of Defense," as the call for applications says. In the current three-year cycle, which runs until 2017, the program expects to disburse $17 million to university-based researchers in the social sciences. Millions more have been allocated since the first round began in 2009.

But there is a substantial difference between research that broadly supports the national interest and work that directly enhances national security. Developing new techniques for teaching Arabic and Chinese, for example, or analyzing EU regulatory policy is the former without necessarily being the latter. When scholars need research money and Washington needs actionable analysis, the danger is that the meaning of the term "national security" can balloon beyond any reasonable definition. Even more worrying, in an

Former U.S. Secretary of State Madeleine Albright delivers a talk at the University of Virginia, February 2013.

era of real transnational threats, knowledge that used to be thought of as the purview of the police—say, how to manage a mass protest and deter crime—can easily slide into matters of surveilling and soldiering.

It was once the case that state-supported research was meant to give the United States an edge in its relations with other countries. Now, with programs such as Minerva, the temptation is to give government an edge over the governed. Recent Minerva projects have focused on the origins of mass political movements, "radicalization" among Somali refugees in Minnesota, and—in the words of one project summary—"the study of Islamic conversion in America," aimed at providing "options for governments to use for the tasking of surveillance." Professors funded by Minerva work with project managers at U.S. military research facilities, who in turn report to the secretary of defense, who has by definition found the research topics to be matters of strategic concern. In an incentive structure that rewards an emphasis on countering global threats and securing the homeland, the devil lies in the definitions. In this framework, the Boston Marathon bombing becomes a national security problem, whereas the Sandy Hook massacre remains a matter for the police and psychologists—a distinction that is both absurd as social science and troubling as public policy.

THE PRICE OF GLOBAL ENGAGEMENT

Things could be different. Funding for foreign-language study, cultural immersion, and advanced inquiry could be a federal priority, with funding levels restored to what they were in previous years. Research and teaching could be placed at one remove from the national security apparatus, as they are in the Department of Education's model for Title VI or in a public trust along the lines of the National Endowment for the Humanities. The creation of knowledge and its communication through instruction could be made immune from "gotcha" politics. And congressional staff members could spend their time on things other than trips to the NSF archives to root out recondite research topics for public ridicule.

At the same time, universities have their own part to play. Disciplines can, and do, go haywire. Researchers and graduate students should be judged not by how well they embed themselves in a scholarly mainstream but by how truly original and world-connected they aim to be. Fundable scholarship should not be reduced to a narrow matter of national security. But it is hard to see why anyone would make a career of international affairs—a pursuit that begins with valuing people, cultures, and polities in all their diversity—without some commitment to serving the public interest.

Given that no one can know where the next crisis will erupt, having a broadly competent reserve of experts is the price of global engagement. Yesterday's apparent irrelevancies—the demographics of eastern Ukraine, for example, or popular attitudes toward public health in West Africa—can suddenly become matters of consequence. Acquiring competence in these sorts of topics forms the mental disposition that J. William Fulbright called "seeing the world as others see it"—an understanding that people could reasonably view their identities, interests, politics, and leaders in ways that might at first seem bizarre or wrong-headed. It also provides the essential context for distinguishing smart policy-specific questions from misguided ones. Great powers should revel in small data: the granular and culture-specific knowledge that can make the critical difference between really getting a place and getting it profoundly wrong.

International affairs education and research are also part of a country's domestic life. Democratic societies depend on having a cadre of informed professionals outside government—people in universities, think tanks, museums, and research institutes who cultivate expertise protected from the pressures of the state. Many countries can field missile launchers and float destroyers; only a few have built a Brookings Institution or a Chatham House. Yet the latter is what makes them magnets for people from the very places their institutions study. The University of London's nearly century-old SOAS, for example, which focuses on Asian and African studies, is a beehive of languages and causes, where Koreans, Nigerians, and Palestinians come to receive world-class instruction on, among other things, North and South Korea, Nigeria, and the Palestinian territories.

All of this points to just how important international and regional studies can be when they are adequately funded, publicly valued, and shielded from the exigencies of national security. Their chief role is not to enable the makers of foreign policy. It is rather to constrain them: to show why things will always be more complicated than they seem, how to foresee unintended consequences, and when to temper ambition with a realistic understanding of what is historically and culturally imaginable. For more than half a century, the world has been shaped by the simple fact that the United States could look at other countries—their pasts and presents, their myths and worldviews—with sympathetic curiosity. Maintaining the ability to do so is not only a great power's insurance policy against the future. It is also the essence of an open, inquisitive, and critical society.

Same as It Ever Was

Why the Techno-optimists Are Wrong

Martin Wolf

Urbanization: Little Italy, Manhattan, circa 1900.

B elief in "the green light, the orgiastic future that year by year recedes before us," as F. Scott Fitzgerald wrote in *The Great Gatsby*, is a characteristic American trait. But hope in a better

---

MARTIN WOLF is Chief Economics Commentator for the *Financial Times*. This article draws on a column he published in the *Financial Times* in 2014.

future is not uniquely American, even if it has long been a more potent secular faith in the United States than elsewhere. The belief has older roots. It was the product of a shift in the temporal location of the golden age from a long-lost past to an ever-brighter future.

That shift was conceived and realized with the Enlightenment and then the Industrial Revolution. As human beings gained ever-greater control of the forces of nature and their economies became ever more productive, they started to hope for lives more like those of the gods their ancestors had imagined.

People might never be immortal, but their lives would be healthy and long. People might never move instantaneously, but they could transport themselves and their possessions swiftly and cheaply across great distances. People might never live on Mount Olympus, but they could enjoy a temperate climate, 24-hour lighting, and abundant food. People might never speak mind to mind, but they could communicate with as many others as they desired, anywhere on the planet. People might never enjoy infinite wisdom, but they could gain immediate access to the knowledge accumulated over millennia.

All of this has already happened in the world's richest countries. It is what the people of the rest of the world hope still to enjoy.

Is a yet more orgiastic future beckoning? Today's Gatsbys have no doubt that the answer is yes: humanity stands on the verge of breakthroughs in information technology, robotics, and artificial intelligence that will dwarf what has been achieved in the past two centuries. Human beings will be able to live still more like gods because they are about to create machines like gods: not just strong and swift but also supremely intelligent and even self-creating.

Yet this is the optimistic version. Since Mary Shelley created the cautionary tale of Frankenstein, the idea of intelligent machines has also frightened us. Many duly point to great dangers, including those of soaring unemployment and inequality.

But are we likely to experience such profound changes over the next decade or two? The answer is no.

SMALL CHANGE

In reality, the pace of economic and social transformation has slowed in recent decades, not accelerated. This is most clearly shown in the rate of growth of output per worker. The economist Robert Gordon, doyen of the skeptics, has noted that the average growth of U.S. output per worker was 2.3 percent a year between 1891 and 1972. Thereafter, it only matched that rate briefly, between 1996 and 2004. It was just 1.4 percent a year between 1972 and 1996 and 1.3 percent between 2004 and 2012.

On the basis of these data, the age of rapid productivity growth in the world's frontier economy is firmly in the past, with only a brief upward blip when the Internet, e-mail, and e-commerce made their initial impact.

Those whom Gordon calls "techno-optimists"—Erik Brynjolfsson and Andrew McAfee of the Massachusetts Institute of Technology, for example—respond that the GDP statistics omit the enormous unmeasured value provided by the free entertainment and information available on the Internet. They emphasize the plethora of cheap or free services (Skype, Wikipedia), the scale of do-it-yourself entertainment (Facebook), and the failure to account fully for all the new products and services. Techno-optimists point out that before June 2007, an iPhone was out of reach for even the richest man on earth. Its price was infinite. The fall from an infinite to a definite price is not reflected in the price indexes. Moreover, say the techno-optimists, the "consumer surplus" in digital products and services—the difference between the price and the value to consumers—is huge. Finally, they argue, measures of GDP underestimate investment in intangible assets.

These points are correct. But they are nothing new: all of this has repeatedly been true since the nineteenth century. Indeed, past innovations generated vastly greater unmeasured value than the relatively trivial innovations of today. Just consider the shift from a world without telephones to one with them, or from a world of oil lamps to one with electric light. Next to that, who cares about Facebook or the iPad? Indeed, who really cares about the Internet when one considers clean water and flushing toilets?

Over the past two centuries, historic breakthroughs have been responsible for generating huge unmeasured value. The motor vehicle eliminated vast quantities of manure from urban streets. The refrigerator prevented food from becoming contaminated. Clean running water and vaccines delivered drastic declines in child mortality rates. The introduction of running water, gas and electric cookers, vacuums, and washing machines helped liberate women from domestic labor. The telephone removed obstacles to speedy contact with the police, fire brigades, and ambulance services. The discovery of electric light eliminated forced idleness. Central heating and air conditioning ended discomfort. The introduction of the railroad, the steam ship, the motor car, and the airplane annihilated distance.

The radio, the gramophone, and the television alone did far more to revolutionize home entertainment than the technologies of the past two decades have. Yet these were but a tiny fraction of the cornucopia of innovation that owed its origin to the so-called general-purpose technologies—industrialized chemistry, electricity, and the internal combustion engine—introduced by what is considered the Second Industrial Revolution, which occurred between the 1870s and the early twentieth century. The reason we are impressed by the relatively paltry innovations of our own time is that we take for granted the innovations of the past.

Gordon also notes how concentrated the period of great breakthroughs was. As he writes:

> Electric light and a workable internal combustion engine were invented in a three-month period in late 1879. The number of municipal waterworks providing fresh running water to urban homes multiplied tenfold between 1870 and 1900. The telephone, phonograph, and motion pictures were all invented in the 1880s.

And the benefits of these mainstays of the Second Industrial Revolution, Gordon points out, "included subsidiary and complementary inventions, from elevators, electric machinery and consumer appliances; to the motorcar, truck, and airplane; to highways, suburbs, and supermarkets; to sewers to carry the wastewater away."

PAST, NOT PROLOGUE

The technologies introduced in the late nineteenth century did more than cause three generations of relatively high productivity growth. They did more, too, than generate huge unmeasured economic and social value. They also brought with them unparalleled social and economic changes. An ancient Roman would have understood the way of life of the United States of 1840 fairly well. He would have found that of 1940 beyond his imagination.

Among the most important of these broader changes were urbanization and the huge jumps in life expectancy and standards of education. The United States was 75 percent rural in the 1870s. By the mid-twentieth century, it was 64 percent urban. Life expectancy rose twice as fast in the first half of the twentieth century as in the second half. The collapse in child mortality is surely the single most beneficial social change of the past two centuries. It is not only a great good in itself; it also liberated women from the burden, trauma, and danger of frequent pregnancies. The jump in high school graduation rates—from less than ten percent of young people in 1900 to roughly 80 percent by 1970—was a central driver of twentieth-century economic growth.

All these changes were also, by their nature, one-offs. This is also true of the more recent shift of women entering the labor force. It has happened. It cannot be repeated.

Yet there is something else of compelling importance in the contrast between the breakthroughs of the nineteenth and early twentieth centuries and those of the second half of the twentieth and the early twenty-first century. The former were vastly broader, affecting energy; transportation; sanitation; food production, distribution, and processing; entertainment; and, not least, entire patterns of habitation. Yes, computers, mobile telecommunications, and the Internet are of great significance. Yet it is also essential to

GEORGE MARKS / GETTY IMAGES

Killer app: vacuuming the den, circa 1950.

remember what has not changed to any fundamental degree. Transportation technologies and speeds are essentially the same as they were half a century ago. The dominant source of commercial energy remains the burning of fossil fuels—introduced with coal and steam in the First Industrial Revolution, of the late eighteenth and early nineteenth centuries—and even nuclear power is now an elderly technology. Although fracking is noteworthy, it does not compare with the opening of the petroleum age in the late nineteenth century.

The only recent connections between homes and the outside world are satellite dishes and broadband. Neither is close to being as important as clean water, sewerage, gas, electricity, and the telephone. The great breakthroughs in health—clean water, sewerage, refrigeration, packaging, vaccinations, and antibiotics—are also all long established.

THE FUTURE'S NOT WHAT IT USED TO BE

The so-called Third Industrial Revolution—of the computer, the Internet, and e-commerce—is also itself quite old. It has already produced many changes. The armies of clerks who used to record all transactions have long since disappeared, replaced by computers; more recently, so have secretaries. E-mail has long since replaced letters. Even the Internet and the technologies that allow it to be searched with ease are now 15 years old, or even older, as is the e-commerce they enabled.

Yet the impact of all of this on measured productivity has been modest. The economic historian Paul David famously argued in 1989 that one should remember how long it took for industrial processes to adapt to electricity. But the computer itself is more than half a century old, and it is now a quarter of a century since David made that point. Yet except for the upward blip between 1996 and 2004, we are still—to adapt the Nobel laureate Robert Solow's celebrated words of 1987—seeing the information technology age "everywhere but in the productivity statistics."

Meanwhile, other, more recent general-purpose technologies—biotechnology and nanotechnology, most notably—have so far made little impact, either economically or more widely.

The disappointing nature of recent growth is also the theme of an influential little book, *The Great Stagnation*, by the economist Tyler Cowen, which is subtitled *How America Ate All the Low-Hanging Fruit of Modern History, Got Sick, and Will (Eventually) Feel Better*. As Cowen writes:

> The American economy has enjoyed . . . low-hanging fruit since at least the seventeenth century, whether it be free land, . . . immigrant labor, or powerful new technologies. Yet during the last 40 years, that low-hanging fruit started disappearing, and we started pretending it was still there. We have failed to recognise that we are at a technological plateau and the trees are more bare than we would like to think. That's it. That is what has gone wrong.

In considering the disappointing impact of recent innovations, it is important to note that the world's economies are vastly bigger than they used to be. Achieving a two percent economy-wide annual rise in labor productivity may simply be a much bigger challenge than it was in the past.

More important, the share of total output of the sectors with the fastest growth in productivity tends to decline over time, while the share of the sectors where productivity growth has

A radio apparatus similar to the one used to transmit the first wireless signal across the Atlantic Ocean, 1901.

proved hardest to increase tends to rise. Indeed, it is possible that productivity growth will essentially cease because the economic contribution of the sectors where it is fastest will become vanishingly small. Raising productivity in manufacturing matters far less now that it generates only about an eighth of total U.S. GDP. Raising productivity in caring for the young, the infirm, the helpless, and the elderly is hard, if not impossible.

Yet perhaps paradoxically, recent technological progress might still have had some important effects on the economy, and particularly the distribution of income, even if its impact on the size of the economy and overall standards of living has been relatively modest. The information age coincided with—and must, to some extent, have caused—adverse economic trends: the stagnation of median real incomes, rising inequality of labor income and of the distribution of income between labor and capital, and growing long-term unemployment.

Information technology has turbocharged globalization by making it vastly easier to organize global supply chains, run 24-hour global financial markets, and spread technological know-how. This has helped accelerate the catch-up process of emerging-market economies, notably China. It has also allowed India to emerge as a significant exporter of technological services.

Technology has also brought about the rise of winner-take-all markets, as superstars have come to bestride the globe. Substantial evidence exists, too, of "skills-biased" technological change. As the demand for and rewards offered to highly skilled workers (software programmers, for example) rise, the demand for and rewards offered to those with skills in the middle of the distribution (such as clerks) decline. The value of intellectual property has also risen. In brief, a modest impact on aggregate output and productivity should not be confused with a modest impact across the board.

NO CRYSTAL BALL REQUIRED

The future is, at least to some extent, unknowable. Yet as Gordon suggests, it is not all that unknowable. Back in the nineteenth and early twentieth centuries, many had already realized the changes that the recent inventions might bring. The nineteenth-century French novelist Jules Verne is a famous example of such foresight.

The optimistic view is that we are now at an inflection point. In their book *The Second Machine Age*, Brynjolfsson and McAfee offer as a parallel the story of the inventor of chess, who asked to be rewarded with one grain of rice on the first square of his board, two on the second, four on the third, and so forth. Manageable in size on the first half of the board, the reward reaches mountainous proportions toward the end of the second. Humanity's reward from Moore's law—the relentless doubling of the number of transistors on a computer chip every two years or so—will, they argue, grow similarly.

These authors predict that we will experience

> two of the most amazing events in history: the creation of true machine intelligence and the connection of all humans via a common digital network, transforming the planet's economics. Innovators, entrepreneurs, scientists, tinkerers, and many other types of geeks will take

advantage of this cornucopia to build technologies that astonish us, delight us, and work for us.

In the near term, however, the widely mentioned possibilities—medicine, even bigger data, robots, 3-D printing, self-driving cars—look quite insignificant.

The impact of the biomedical advances so far has been remarkably small, with pharmaceutical companies finding it increasingly difficult to register significant breakthroughs. So-called big data is clearly helping decision-making. But many of its products—ultra-high-speed trading, for example—are either socially and economically irrelevant or, quite possibly, harmful. Three-D printing is a niche activity—fun, but unlikely to revolutionize manufacturing.

Making robots replicate all the complex abilities of human beings has proved extremely difficult. Yes, robots can do well-defined human jobs in well-defined environments. Indeed, it is quite possible that standard factory work will be entirely automated. But the automation of such work is already very far advanced. It is not a revolution in the making. Yes, it is possible to imagine driverless cars. But this would be a far smaller advance than were cars themselves.

Inevitably, uncertainty is pervasive. Many believe that the impact of what is still to come could be huge. The economist Carl Benedikt Frey and the machine-learning expert Michael Osborne, both of Oxford University, have concluded that 47 percent of U.S. jobs are at high risk from automation. In the nineteenth century, they argue, machines replaced artisans and benefited unskilled labor. In the twentieth century, computers replaced middle-income jobs, creating a polarized labor market.

Over the next decades, they write, "most workers in transportation and logistics occupations, together with the bulk of office and administrative support workers, and labour in production occupations, are likely to be substituted by computer capital." Moreover, they add, "computerisation will mainly substitute for low-skill and low-wage jobs in the near future. By contrast, high-skill and high-wage occupations are the least susceptible to computer capital."

That would exacerbate already existing trends toward greater inequality. But remember that previous advances also destroyed millions of jobs. The most striking example is, of course, in agriculture, which was the dominant employer of humanity between the dawn of the agricultural revolution and the nineteenth century.

The economists Jeffrey Sachs and Laurence Kotlikoff even argue that the rise in productivity generated by the coming revolution could make future generations worse off in the aggregate. The replacement of workers by robots could shift income from the former to the robots' owners, most of whom will be retired, and the retired are assumed to save less than the young. This would lower investment in human capital because the young could no longer afford to pay for it, and it would lower investment in machines because savings in this economy would fall.

Beyond this, people imagine something far more profound than robots able to do gardening and the like: the "technological singularity," when intelligent machines take off in a rapid cycle of self-improvement, leaving mere human beings behind. In this view, we will someday create machines with the abilities once ascribed to gods. Is that imminent? I have no idea.

BEEN THERE, DONE THAT

So how might we respond now to these imagined futures?

First, new technologies bring good and bad. We must believe we can shape the good and manage the bad.

Second, we must understand that education is not a magic wand. One reason is that we do not know what skills will be demanded three decades hence. Also, if Frey and Osborne are right, so many low- to middle-skilled jobs are at risk that it may already be too late for anybody much over 18 and for many children. Finally, even if the demand for creative, entrepreneurial, and high-level knowledge services were to grow on the required scale, which is highly unlikely, turning us all into the happy few is surely a fantasy.

Third, we will have to reconsider leisure. For a long time, the wealthiest lived a life of leisure at the expense of the toiling masses.

The rise of intelligent machines would make it possible for many more people to live such lives without exploiting others. Today's triumphant puritanism finds such idleness abhorrent. Well then, let people enjoy themselves busily. What else is the true goal of the vast increases in prosperity we have created?

Fourth, we may need to redistribute income and wealth on a large scale. Such redistribution could take the form of a basic income for every adult, together with funding for education and training at any stage in a person's life. In this way, the potential for a more enjoyable life might become a reality. The revenue could come from taxes on bads (pollution, for example) or on rents (including land and, above all, intellectual property). Property rights are a social creation. The idea that a small minority should overwhelmingly benefit from new technologies should be reconsidered. It would be possible, for example, for the state to obtain an automatic share of the income from the intellectual property it protects.

Fifth, if labor shedding does accelerate, it will be essential to ensure that demand for labor expands in tandem with the rise in potential supply. If we succeed, many of the worries over a lack of jobs will fade away. Given the failure to achieve this in the past seven years, that may well not happen. But we could do better if we wanted to.

The rise of truly intelligent machines, if it comes, would indeed be a big moment in history. It would change many things, including the global economy. Their potential is clear: they would, in principle, make it possible for human beings to live far better lives. Whether they end up doing so depends on how the gains are produced and distributed.

It is also possible that the ultimate result might be a tiny minority of huge winners and a vast number of losers. But such an outcome would be a choice, not a destiny. Techno-feudalism is unnecessary. Above all, technology itself does not dictate the outcomes. Economic and political institutions do. If the ones we have do not give the results we want, we will need to change them.

As for the singularity, it is hard to conceive of such a state of the world. Would a surpassed humanity live happily ever after, tended, like children, by solicitous machines? Would people find meaning in a world in which their intellectual progeny were so vastly superior to themselves?

What we know for the moment is that there is nothing extraordinary in the changes we are now experiencing. We have been here before and on a much larger scale. But the current and prospective rounds of changes still create problems—above all, the combination of weak growth and significant increases in inequality. The challenge, as always, is to manage such changes. The only good reason to be pessimistic is that we are doing such a poor job of this.

The future does not have to be a disappointment. But as Gatsby learned, it can all too easily be just that.

The End of Pax Americana

Why Washington's Middle East Pullback Makes Sense

Steven Simon and Jonathan Stevenson

Don't look back: U.S. soldiers leaving Iraq, December 2011.

STEVEN SIMON is a Visiting Lecturer at Dartmouth College and served as Senior Director for Middle Eastern and North African Affairs at the White House from 2011 through 2012.

JONATHAN STEVENSON is Professor of Strategic Studies at the U.S. Naval War College and served as Director for Political-Military Affairs for the Middle East and North Africa on the U.S. National Security Council staff from 2011 to 2013.

The Obama administration has clearly pulled back from the United States' recent interventionism in the Middle East, notwithstanding the rise of the Islamic State (also known as ISIS) and the U.S.-led air war against it. Critics pin the change on the administration's aversion to U.S. activism in the region, its unwillingness to engage in major combat operations, or President Barack Obama's alleged ideological preference for diminished global engagement. But the reality is that Washington's post-9/11 interventions in the region—especially the one in Iraq—were anomalous and shaped false perceptions of a "new normal" of American intervention, both at home and in the region. The administration's unwillingness to use ground forces in Iraq or Syria constitutes not so much a withdrawal as a correction—an attempt to restore the stability that had endured for several decades thanks to American restraint, not American aggressiveness.

It's possible to argue that pulling back is less a choice than a necessity. Some realist observers claim that in a time of economic uncertainty and cuts to the U.S. military budget, an expansive U.S. policy in the region has simply become too costly. According to that view, the United States, like the United Kingdom before it, is the victim of its own "imperial overstretch." Others argue that U.S. policy initiatives, especially the recent negotiations with Iran over its nuclear program, have distanced Washington from its traditional Middle Eastern allies; in other words, the United States isn't pulling back so much as pushing away.

The long period of American primacy in the Middle East is ending.

In actuality, however, the main driver of the U.S. pullback is not what's happening in Washington but what's happening in the region. Political and economic developments in the Middle East have reduced the opportunities for effective American intervention to a vanishing point, and policymakers in Washington have been recognizing that and acting accordingly. Given this, the moderate U.S. pullback should be not reversed but rather continued, at least in the absence of a significant threat to core U.S. interests.

BACK TO NORMAL

Between World War II and the 9/11 attacks, the United States was the quintessential status quo power in the Middle East, undertaking military intervention in the region only in exceptional circumstances. Direct U.S. military involvement was nonexistent, minimal, or indirect in the 1948 Arab-Israeli war, the 1956 Suez crisis, the Six-Day War in 1967, the Yom Kippur War in 1973, and the Iran-Iraq War in the 1980s. The 1982–84 U.S. peacekeeping mission in Lebanon was a notorious failure and gave rise to the "overwhelming force" doctrine, which precluded subsequent U.S. interventions until Saddam Hussein's extraordinarily reckless invasion of Kuwait forced Washington's hand in 1990.

Washington didn't need a forward-leaning policy because U.S. interests largely coincided with those of its strategic allies and partners in the region and could be served through economic and diplomatic relations combined with a modest military presence. The United States and the Gulf Arab states shared a paramount need to

CAROLYN KASTER / POOL / REUTERS

U.S. Defense Secretary Ash Carter arrives at King Abdulaziz International Airport in Jeddah, Saudi Arabia, July 2015.

maintain stable oil supplies and prices and, more broadly, political stability. Since the Iranian Revolution in 1979, the United States, Israel, and the Gulf Arab states have had the mutual objective of containing Iran. Beginning with the Camp David accords in 1978, American, Egyptian, and Israeli interests converged, and their trilateral relationship was reinforced by substantial U.S. aid to Egypt and Israel alike. And even after 9/11, the United States, Israel, and the Gulf Arab states had shared priorities in their fights against terrorism.

Over the past decade, however, several factors largely unrelated to Washington's own policy agenda have weakened the bases for these alliances and partnerships. First, the advent of hydraulic fracturing has dramatically reduced direct U.S. dependence on Gulf oil and diminished the strategic value and priority of the U.S. relationship with Saudi Arabia and the smaller Gulf Arab states: indeed, the United States will soon overtake Saudi Arabia as the world's largest producer of crude oil and will need to import less fossil fuel. Although Gulf producers will keep determining the world price of oil and U.S. companies will continue to have a stake in the Gulf's wells, the United States will enjoy greater policy discretion and flexibility.

The spread and intensification of jihadism have also weakened the strategic links between the United States and its regional partners. A decade ago, a combination of American pressure and the shock of large-scale al Qaeda attacks inside Saudi Arabia convinced the Saudis and their neighbors to clamp down on jihadist activities within their own borders. Yet today, the Gulf Arab states have subordinated the suppression of jihadism to the goal of overthrowing Syrian President Bashar al-Assad and hobbling his patrons in Iran. They are doing this by backing Sunni extremist rebels in Syria despite Washington's exhortations to stop and Saudi Arabia's own desire to avoid a post-Assad Syria ruled by radicals. The United States' regional partners see themselves as less and less answerable to Washington, and Washington feels less obligated to protect the interests of those partners, which seem increasingly parochial and remote from

American interests and values. In addition, widespread Islamic radicalization has driven the emergence of a genuine pan-Islamic identity that complicates Western involvement in the Middle East. Consider, for example, the unwillingness of many moderate Sunni Syrian opponents of Assad to accept European or U.S. help, which they believe will disqualify them in the eyes of Islamists.

Meanwhile, from the United States' standpoint, the Middle East has become a highly dubious place to invest owing to systemic political and economic dysfunction. The region features little water, sparse agriculture, and a massive oversupply of labor. Of the Middle Eastern countries that still function, most run large fiscal and external deficits, maintain huge and inefficient civil service payrolls, and heavily subsidize fuel and other necessities for their populations; lower oil revenues will probably limit the Gulf states' ability to finance those creaky mechanisms. Active conflicts in many Middle Eastern states have displaced large proportions of their populations and deprived their young people of educational opportunities and hope for the future. These conditions have produced either abject despair or, what is more ominous, political and religious radicalization. The effort to remake the Middle East as an incubator of liberal democracy that would pacify young Muslims failed even when the United States had plenty of cash to throw at the project and more reasons for optimism about its prospects, in the years immediately following the 9/11 attacks.

Finally, groups within Middle Eastern societies that were once reliable bastions of pro-Western sentiment—such as national militaries, oil-industry elites, and secular technocrats—have generally seen their influence wane. And in instances where traditional pro-Western elements have retained power, their interests and policies now increasingly diverge from American ones. The Egyptian military, for example, served for decades as a pillar of the U.S.-Egyptian relationship. Thanks to the coup it launched in 2013 that placed the former army general Abdel Fattah el-Sisiat the top of a new authoritarian regime, the military now exerts more control than ever in Egypt. But this hardly augurs well for Washington: if past is prologue, the military's brutal suppression of the Muslim Brotherhood will almost certainly lead to an increase in jihadist violence and thus expose the United States to the very blowback that its assistance to Egypt is intended to prevent. Hopes in the 1950s and 1960s for the ascendance of a secular, technocratic, Western-oriented Arab elite that would bring their societies with them have long since faded.

POWERFUL BUT POWERLESS

At the same time that the salience of the Middle East to U.S. policy is waning and the interests of the United States and its traditional partners in the Middle East are diverging, the potential for American military power to effect major change in the region is also diminishing. The decentralization of al Qaeda and the emergence of ISIS, a jihadist expeditionary force and quasi state, have increased the asymmetries between U.S. military capabilities and the most urgent threats facing the region. As U.S.-occupied Iraq slid toward civil war in 2006, the Pentagon moved toward improving U.S. counterinsurgency doctrine and practice, revamping the military's structure to emphasize irregular warfare and special operations. But liberal and accountable democratic governments find it difficult to marshal either the staying power or the savagery that is usually required to suppress an unruly and committed indigenous group— especially a regionwide social movement such as ISIS, which does not recognize physical or political boundaries. This is particularly true when outside powers have no local partners with substantial bureaucratic cohesion or popular legitimacy. The United States still has the resources and resilience to sustain wars against modern nationalist states that would end with clear victors and enforceable outcomes. But Americans have learned the hard way that a transnational clash of ethnicities turbocharged by religious narratives is vastly harder to navigate, let alone manipulate.

A U.S.-led military operation against ISIS, for instance, would no doubt produce impressive and gratifying battlefield victories. But the aftermath of the conflict would drive home the ultimate futility of the project. Solidifying any tactical gains would require political will backed by the support of the American public; a large cadre of deployable civilian experts in reconstruction and stabilization; deep knowledge of the society for whose fate a victorious United States would take responsibility; and, most problematic, a sustained military force to provide security for populations and infrastructure. Even if all those conditions were present, Washington would struggle to find dependable and dedicated local constituents or clients, or indeed allies, to assist. If this sounds familiar, it is because it is the same list of things that Washington wasn't able to put together the last two times it launched major military interventions in the Middle East, with the invasion of Iraq in 2003 and the NATO air campaign against Libya in 2011. Put simply, the United States would likely lose another war in the Middle East for all the same reasons it lost the last two.

Even a less intensive, counterterrorism-based approach to ISIS, which would involve steady drone strikes and periodic commando operations, would carry grave risks. Collateral damage from U.S. drone attacks, for example, has made it harder for the Pakistani government to extend deeper cooperation to the United States. Five years ago, U.S. military officials took great pride in special operations raids in Afghanistan that resulted in the death or capture of high-value Taliban operatives. But the civilian casualties the raids produced undermined strategic goals by enraging locals and driving them back into the Taliban's orbit.

For these reasons, U.S. policymakers should entertain serious doubts about taking ownership of any of the Middle East's ongoing conflicts. Precisely those kinds of doubts explain and justify the Obama administration's unwillingness to intervene more forcefully in Syria. For a period in 2012 and early 2013, the administration considered a full range of options for Syria, including U.S.-enforced no-fly and buffer zones, regime change by force (facilitated by far more substantial American and allied military assistance to anti-Assad rebels), and limited retaliatory air strikes against the regime in response to its use of chemical weapons. But the growing involvement of Iran's Islamic Revolutionary Guard Corps and the Lebanese Shiite militia Hezbollah in defending Assad would have meant an unabashed U.S. proxy war with Iran that could have escalated and spilled over into the rest of region. That would have made it impossible to carry on fruitful talks with Tehran about curtailing its nuclear program and would have forced the United States to surpass Iran's high levels of commitment and investment in the conflict. In addition, a U.S.-led intervention would have enjoyed very little international backing: China and Russia would have vetoed any UN resolution authorizing it, just as they had vetoed far less muscular resolutions, and the Arab League and NATO would not have endorsed it. And major Western military action would likely have intensified the spread of jihadism in Syria, as it had elsewhere.

KEEP CALM AND CARRY ON

The United States' primary interest in the Middle East is regional stability. For now at least, constraints on U.S. power and the complex, interdependent nature of U.S. interests in the region—as well as the likelihood of sustained U.S.-Chinese rivalry that will inevitably divert U.S. strategic attention to the Asia-Pacific region— suggest that the best Middle East policy for Washington would be something closer to what international relations theorists call "offshore balancing": refraining from engagement in overseas military operations and forgoing quasi-imperial nation building to focus instead on selectively using its considerable leverage to exert influence and protect U.S. interests. Washington needs to husband U.S. power in the Middle East, unless a genuine existential threat to its regional allies arises, which is unlikely. This course will require Washington to avoid any further projection of U.S. military power in the region—for example, a large-scale deployment of combat ground troops to fight ISIS.

Critics of U.S. restraint argue that in the absence of strongly asserted U.S. power, Iran or other U.S. nemeses will be emboldened—that restraint will lead to war. But U.S. adversaries will likely judge Washington's resolve on the basis of conditions as they appear in the moment those adversaries are seriously considering aggressive actions, irrespective of conditions that existed years or months before. As long as the limits of U.S. restraint are clearly enunciated and Washington makes plain that its alliance with Israel remains undiminished, Iran will be loath to confront Israel or act much more aggressively in Iraq, Syria, Yemen, or elsewhere in the region for fear of triggering a decisive American response that could scupper the nuclear deal and revive the painful sanctions that drove Tehran to the bargaining table in the first place. In any case, the question of whether saber rattling will provoke or deter a potential adversary can never be answered with complete confidence, since decision-makers often misjudge the perceptions and temperament of their rivals.

> U.S. policymakers should entertain serious doubts about taking ownership of any of the Middle East's ongoing conflicts.

Whether rapprochement is a promising paradigm for U.S.-Iranian relations remains to be seen. Iran clearly seeks to exert its influence wherever it can, but it's far from clear that it can dominate the region. Iranian influence in Iraq was aided by the vacuum created by the U.S. invasion but stems more broadly from the demographic and political primacy of Iraq's Shiites and is thus unavoidable. As long as Baghdad remains dependent on the United States for countering ISIS, Washington should retain sufficient leverage to moderate Iraqi politics and limit Iran's sway. Iranian support for the Houthi rebels in Yemen and for dissident Shiites in Bahrain is more opportunistic than strategic and therefore unlikely to permanently shift the balance of power in either place. Tehran's meddling in the Israeli-Palestinian conflict doesn't rise to the level of a strategic challenge: the Palestinian militant group Hamas has not been able to translate Iranian largess into a serious advantage over Israel, let alone Egypt and the Palestinian Authority, all of which oppose Hamas. Iran's footholds in Lebanon and Syria go back decades, but even though its proxies in both places have steadily increased their commitment to defend the Assad regime, they have been unable to avert Syria's de facto partition. Even if Iran chooses to make Syria its Vietnam, the best it could probably manage against an externally supported anti-Assad opposition would be to consolidate the status quo while sharing the meager rewards with Moscow. Syria, then, would be a springboard for Iranian mischief but hardly a platform for controlling the region. In short, even with the nuclear deal in place, Iran won't be able to do much more now—and possibly even less—than it was able to do in the past.

The nuclear deal has produced a genuine split between the Americans and the Israelis, who believe that the deal's terms are too lenient and won't prevent the Iranians from developing a nuclear weapon. But the divide is unlikely to have dire practical consequences. Washington has an obligation to maintain its unique relationship with Israel and has a strategic interest in preserving bilateral links with the Israeli military, which is by far the region's most powerful fighting force. The nuclear deal with Iran also upset the Gulf Arab states. But Washington's global economic responsibilities and its substantial counterterrorist interests still require the United States to safeguard its strategic relationship with those countries, particularly Saudi Arabia. And the Gulf Arab states retain a stronger cultural connection with the United States than with any other major power: Gulf elites send their children to American universities as opposed to Chinese, Russian, or European ones.

The Israelis and the Gulf Arabs need not panic: prudence dictates a serviceable regional U.S. military presence to prevent ISIS from expanding further (into Jordan, for example) and to deter Iranian breaches of the nuclear deal and respond to any destabilizing Iranian moves, such as a major ground intervention in Iraq. The American military footprint in the region should not change. At least one U.S. carrier battle group should remain assigned to the Arabian Sea. The structure and personnel strength of U.S. military bases in the Middle East should stay the same. The air campaign against ISIS should continue, and American troops will still need to be deployed occasionally on a selective basis to quell terrorist threats or even respond in a limited way to large-scale atrocities or environmental disasters. But a resolute policy of restraint requires that any major expeditionary military ground intervention on the part of the United States in the Middle East be avoided and that regional partners be encouraged to take on more responsibility for their own security.

AIM LOWER, SCORE HIGHER

In addition to affirming its pullback from the military interventionism of the post-9/11 era, Washington needs to recalibrate its diplomatic priorities. The aftermath of the Arab revolts of 2011—especially those in Egypt, Libya, and Syria—demonstrated that most Middle Eastern societies are not ready to take significant steps toward democracy, and so American attempts to promote further political liberalization in the region should be more subdued. U.S. officials should also recognize that a lasting peace between Israel and the Palestinians is highly unlikely to take shape in the medium term. The United States' dogged determination to accomplish that objective, even in the least propitious circumstances, has created a moral hazard. Successive Israeli governments have been able to thwart Washington's peacemaking efforts with near impunity, confident that the Americans would continue to try no matter what. In turn, the United States' inability to facilitate an agreement has contributed to perceptions of Washington as a declining power—even as some U.S. allies in the Gulf see U.S. pressure on Israel as another example of U.S. faithlessness as an ally.

The United States should always support the goals of democratization and Israeli-Palestinian peace. But in the medium term, rather than unrealistically clinging to those aims, Washington should try to capitalize on the Iran nuclear deal to improve relations with Tehran. If the implementation of the deal gets off to a relatively smooth start, Washington should probe Tehran's flexibility in other areas with an eye to fostering a kind of modus vivendi between the Iranians and the Saudis—something that looks very unlikely now, as it has for years. One way to do so would be to bring Iran and other governments together in an effort to end the Syrian civil war through a political agreement. The emerging recognition among the major players—the United States, Russia, Iran, and the Gulf Arab states—is that, although ISIS' dream of a border-busting caliphate remains out of the group's reach, the ongoing conflict in Syria risks dangerously empowering ISIS and accelerating the propagation of its extremist ideology.

But each player has also come to realize that its preferred method of solving the Syrian crisis is probably unworkable. For the United States and its Gulf partners, supporting forcible regime change by Syrian rebels who are increasingly infiltrated or co-opted by ISIS appears counterproductive as well as operationally dubious. At the same time, after more than four years of a military stalemate, it is clear that Iran's ongoing support for Assad and Russia's recent intensification of its aid to the regime can merely help maintain the status quo but cannot decisively swing conditions in Assad's favor. Both Tehran and Moscow seem to understand that regardless of their support, Assad's regime is weaker than ever and it will probably prove impossible to reconstitute a unitary Syria ruled exclusively by the regime. For mainly these reasons, both Iran and Russia have recently shown more interest in exploring a negotiated settlement. Although Russia's protestations that it is not wedded to Assad are disingenuous, Moscow has supported the UN Security Council's investigation of the regime's apparent use of indiscriminate barrel bombs filled with poisonous chlorine gas and has backed the Security Council's August 2015 statement reinvigorating the quest for a political transition in Syria. Tehran, with Hezbollah's support, has been pushing a peace plan involving a national unity government and a revised constitution, although one under which Assad or his regime would remain in power at least in the short term.

A realistic mechanism for taking advantage of these tenuously converging interests has not materialized. But the Iran nuclear deal has demonstrated the potential of diplomacy to ameliorate regional crises. In addition to countering the spread of jihadism, a

U.S.-brokered agreement to end the Syrian civil war would mitigate and eventually end the world's most pressing humanitarian crisis and restore much of the American prestige that has waned in the region. Effective and inclusive conflict resolution on Syria would also validate the rapprochement with Iran and might help convince the Israelis of the efficacy of the United States' new approach.

Washington should leverage the new diplomatic bonds that the nuclear negotiations forged among the major powers—and, in particular, between U.S. and Iranian officials—to reinvigorate multinational talks on Syria's transition. An initial step might be to reconvene the Geneva II conference, which foundered in February 2014, gathering the original parties and adding Iran to the mix. Russia's insistence that Assad's departure cannot be a precondition to political talks should not be a deal breaker and in fact could be an enticement for Iran to participate, which U.S. Secretary of State John Kerry might now be able to facilitate through a direct appeal to Iranian Foreign Minister Mohammad Javad Zarif. The Gulf Arab states' cautious endorsement of the nuclear agreement and Saudi Arabia's participation in trilateral talks with the United States and Russia on Syria in early August suggest that the Gulf Arabs are growing more comfortable with diplomacy as a means of easing strategic tensions with Iran. On account of their heightened perception of the ISIS threat, Qatar, Saudi Arabia, and Turkey might now drop their insistence that Assad depart prior to negotiations.

The hardest part, of course, will be arriving at plausible transitional arrangements. One possibility would be to create a power-sharing body with executive authority that could marginalize ISIS and Jabhat al-Nusra, the Syria-based militant group affiliated with al Qaeda, as implicitly contemplated in the August UN Security Council statement. Another would be to partition the country to some degree and establish a confederacy of sorts to replace central rule from Damascus. Tactical cease-firesreached between the regime and moderate opposition forces could serve as the building blocks for those kinds of broader political arrangements and might also allow the parties to focus on fighting the jihadist factions, which represent a common enemy.

MATURE WITHDRAWAL

The long period of American primacy in the Middle East is ending. Although the Iraq war damaged Washington's credibility and empowered U.S. adversaries, by the time the United States invaded Iraq, the region was already becoming less malleable all on its own. The United States should not and cannot withdraw in a literal sense, but it should continue to pull back, both to service strategic priorities elsewhere and in recognition of its dwindling influence. Neither the United States nor its regional partners want to see Iran with nuclear weapons or substantially increased regional influence. And none of the main players in the region wants to see a quantum leap in the power of ISIS or other Salafi jihadist organizations. But because the United States' leverage has diminished, it must concentrate on forging regional stability. That would be a wiser approach than pushing for improbable political liberalization and a resolution to the Israeli-Palestinian conflict, as the Obama administration has done, or trying to transform the region through the use of force, a strategy that the Bush administration relied on with woeful results.

In particular, Washington must acknowledge that reducing its military role will mean that its allies will exercise greater independence in their own military decisions. In turn, U.S. allies need to understand just how much support Washington is willing to provide before they launch risky military adventures, such as Saudi Arabia's recent strikes against the Houthi rebels in Yemen. Washington and its partners need better bilateral and multilateral communications and planning. Washington will need to be clearer about what might prompt it to intervene militarily and what level of force it would use, and it will need to initiate more detailed joint planning for the full range of its possible responses.

Israel still favors confronting Iran instead of smoothing relations, and Washington will have to strictly police the nuclear deal to convince the Israelis of its effectiveness. But as ISIS has risen, the Gulf Arab states and Turkey have warmed a bit to the United States' approach to Iran and to Washington's position that containing the spread of jihadism is now more important than achieving regime change in Syria.

For Washington to successfully commit itself to a constructive pullback from the Middle East, it will need to make its best efforts to avoid directly impeding the priorities of its regional allies and partners—and it should demand that its friends in the region do the same. That will require focused diplomacy supported by clear articulations of Washington's commitment to its core interests. Washington should stress, in particular, that the Iran nuclear deal will actually ensure, rather than threaten, sustained U.S. diplomatic engagement in the region. Instead of reversing course, Washington needs to embrace the idea of establishing a healthier equilibrium in U.S.–Middle Eastern relations, one that involves a lighter management role for the United States. The military-centric interventionism of the past 14 years was an aberration from a longer history of American restraint; it must not harden into a new long-term norm.

China's Boyfriends for Hire

How to Survive the Chinese New Year

Clarissa Sebag-Montefiore

Women in wedding gowns participate in a brides' race event for the Qixi Festival in Guangzhou, August 12, 2013.

C hina's largest online marketplace, Taobao, offers everything from inflatable donkeys to live mice to breast implants. And now fake boyfriends are available for purchase, too.

CLARISSA SEBAG-MONTEFIORE is a British journalist who lived in China from 2009 to 2014, during which time she worked as an editor for *Time Out Beijing* and *Time Out Shanghai*.

Men offer their companionship for as little as 1,000 yuan ($160) to as much as 10,000 yuan ($1,599) a day—and even charge extra for romantic activities such as handholding, going to the cinema together, cuddles, or joint Internet surfing (yes, even that).

But the "rent-a-boyfriends" aren't really for lonely hearts. More commonly, women, usually in their late twenties and up, hire them to put on an act for their parents—a novel way for them to stave off marriage pressure.

This week marks the Chinese New Year—when that pressure reaches a boiling point. As millions of rural-to-urban migrants return home to celebrate China's most important holiday, legions of unmarried women will be lectured by extended family about their singlehood. Enter the burgeoning rent-a-boyfriend industry.

Although the exact number of renters is hard to come by, and it is still considered a last resort, there is certainly rising interest in the industry. Online searches for the term "rental boyfriend" rose by 884 percent between 2012 and 2013, **according to Taobao.** Although there are also girlfriends for rent, a quick look online shows that the majority of people advertising themselves as fake partners are male.

This imbalance may seem surprising given that in China, cultural preference for boys has skewed the birthrate. **At its peak in** 2004, 121.2 boys were born to every 100 girls. That figure dropped slightly in 2013 to 117.6. Still, it is estimated that there will be a surplus of up to 30 million young men in China by 2020. Most of these bachelors, however, live in the impoverished countryside. In major cities, it is often the women struggling to find a match (and it is urban women who can afford to rent boyfriends).

Hypergamy, the expectation in China that women should "marry up" financially and in status, has left many of the country's most educated, successful professional women without a mate. **According to the Brookings-Tsinghua Center for Public Policy in Beijing,** in urban areas there are an estimated seven million unmarried women between the ages of 25 and 34. Around seven percent of college-aged women remain single until they are 45. Some have struggled to find love; others have chosen to delay marriage for their careers. Either way, if unmarried by the age of 27, they are dubbed *sheng nu*—literally "leftover women." (The prefix *sheng* is derived from the same word used for "leftover food" and reflects the disdain with which this nickname is used.)

There is, however, a small grace period for these *sheng nu*. Initially, they are considered "holy warriors," with some fight left to find a husband. But if they are still single by the age of 31, they become "a leftover as high as heaven"—considered by many to be too old to marry.

To avoid this fate, pressure for girls to marry starts early. In 2012, best-selling writer Wang Hailing, author of *Divorce with Chinese Characteristics,* relayed stories on her microblog about pushy mothers. In one account, a single girl said to her mother, "What's the rush? I'm only 23." The mother replied in turn: "Only? If you're a boy you can claim 'only,' for girls it's 'already'!"

"One of my friends tried a variety of ways to persuade her daughter to go on a blind date," Wang wrote in another post. "Nagging her/going on about the importance for girls to get married in their 'valuable' age. If they don't take their chance now, then they will either be leftovers, or on sale!"

Leta Hong Fincher, author of *Leftover Women: The Resurgence of Gender Inequality in China,* recalls interviewing one woman whose mother refused to talk to her—going so far as to reject her daughter's phone calls—until she found herself a boyfriend. Fincher sees this behavior as part of "a real tradition of tremendous pain, burden, and guilt." Unmarried women are not only an embarrassment for parents but are also seen as less able to provide for them financially.

The pressure on women to marry dates to ancient times. Confucian ideals stress that marriage is a matter not of individual desire but of duty: filial daughters are expected to produce grandchildren. But the generation born in the 1980s and 1990s under the one-child policy has an even bigger burden. Those young adults must shoulder a load of parental expectations that rests on them alone. And in a country with a thin to nonexistent state welfare system, stable marriages are seen as a necessity in providing for retired parents and in-laws.

"Han women traditionally had their feet bound, they were meant to stay in the house, they were meant to breed and give heirs to their husbands," Jemimah Steinfeld, author of the new book *Little Emperors and Material Girls: Sex and Youth in Modern China,* told me. In China today, she said, the soaring skyscrapers and bold architecture merely hide these stubborn old customs. "A man can be many things in modern China. A woman is still seen as someone who is meant to conform at some stage. There is a tradition and history that is hard to shake off."

For China's younger generations, however, love is now part of the marriage equation. Many women no longer see settling as an option. Fed with a diet of Western and Chinese rom-coms and pop songs, they now want chemistry, romance, and love. For that they are willing to wait: in 2012, Shanghai announced that the median age for brides topped 30 years for the first time ever.

But in order to delay marriage, women must battle not just familial expectations but the Chinese state. *Sheng nu* became official lexicon in 2007 when it was listed by the Chinese Ministry of Education as one of 171 new words. Meanwhile, the All China Women's Federation, a government body founded to promote women's rights, published an article in 2011 titled "Leftover Women Do Not Deserve Our Sympathy." Girls might "hope to further their education in order to increase their competitiveness," the article declared. "The tragedy is, they don't realize that as women age, they are worth less and less. So by the time they get their M.A. or Ph.D. they are already old—like yellowed pearls." And it is not only the All China Women's Federation that is pushing for rings on fingers but also state media, universities, work units (for whom holding matchmaking events is a matter of course), and even the medical establishment.

Fincher believes that endemic derision of unmarried women is tied in to the government's emphasis on the family as the cornerstone of Chinese society. Legions of single women and men might lead to social disorder, so the thinking goes. "There are People's Daily editorials warning specifically about the threat to social stability, about men not being able to find brides, that they get involved in criminal activities, cause trouble," explains Fincher. "The single women choosing to delay marriage for education or career are [also] not conforming to their traditional roles and they are not having a child, which is their biological duty from the point of view of the government."

As such, Fincher told me that she has noticed a "continuous aggressive push to stigmatize these single, educated professional women as *sheng nu*," one that is difficult or near impossible to ignore. "Even if the women themselves just brush off the messages in the media, their parents may well accept it. There is very much a collective sense of marriage anxiety surrounding these women."

No doubt there are a handful of women renting boyfriends who hope for some real connection—or at least a release for a few hours or days from being alone. Today's younger generations in China are often only children, thousands of miles away from their parents, living in soulless high-rise buildings and working crushingly long hours.

But for most, renting a boyfriend—or, in extreme cases, going so far as to hire a "husband" (there have been one or two cases of this, too)—is a byproduct of a society where saving face is crucial. "It's about fitting into these roles. To appear to be doing it so you don't cause chaos," Steinfeld explained. "So long as that is how it looks, it doesn't matter if that is not how it is. Rent a boyfriend—yes, it is superficial. But in China the superficial matters. Playing that part is important."

Weed World

Lessons from Marijuana Legalization Around the Globe

John Collins

AMIR COHEN / REUTERS

A worker harvests cannabis plants at a plantation near the Israeli city of Nazareth, May 28, 2013.

I n the blink of an eye, global debates about cannabis regulation have shifted from "whether" to "how." In 2014, Uruguay became the first nation to explicitly regulate cannabis from seed to sale. Its preferred strategy? State-regulated production, cannabis clubs,

JOHN COLLINS is coordinator of the LSE IDEAS International Drug Policy Project.

and personal growing. Meanwhile, four U.S. states and the District of Columbia have moved ahead with legal regulation, Colorado and Washington being the first, and the federal government seems unlikely to intervene. More states, possibly even California, look set to follow. Likewise, in the rest of the world, there are a number of gray-area regulatory systems, including in Belgium, the Netherlands, and Spain. All offer insights into how the United States—and other countries—might tackle the "how."

THE AMERICAN MODEL

In 2015, researchers at RAND produced an exhaustive study on cannabis legalization. The core insight was that "legalization is not simply a binary choice between making the production, sale, and possession of the drug legal on the one hand and continuing existing prohibitions on the other." The report's authors suggest that, if states do pursue legalization, a state monopoly, in which the government controls price, production methods, and quantities produced, is likely the most attractive supply model. Drug policy experts Professor Mark Kleiman and Jeremy Ziskind offer a similar analysis in their contribution to the London School of Economics Expert Group on the Economics of Drug Policy Report, writing, "The debate over how to legalise cannabis tends to assume that for-profit commercial enterprise is the default option. Legalising cannabis on the alcohol model may, however, be the second-worst option (behind only continued prohibition)."

Legalization regimes have two facets: rules for medical marijuana and rules for recreational marijuana. In the United States, states have opted for a spectrum of models to deal with medical marijuana. Some states' medical laws are considered so lenient as to constitute de facto legalization, for example in parts of California. New Jersey and New York, due to regulatory design or a lack of support from their governors, have witnessed a bumpier rollout and greater restrictions on supply and qualifying ailments. New Jersey Governor Chris Christie has made clear his lack of support for medical marijuana, and he initially stalled implementation.

Meanwhile, New York State, viewed as having the strictest regulations in the country, has a long implementation process that will stretch into 2016. New York Governor Andrew Cuomo has overseen continued protests, most notably from parents of sick children suffering from a range of illnesses, from brain tumors to seizure disorders, over the slow progress.

The patchwork applies to recreational cannabis as well. Colorado has taken a soft regulatory touch and transformed many of its well-run medical cannabis businesses into recreational providers. These are balanced by a strong state tax regime aiming to fund new public works, such as schools and anti-drug educational programs. Its regulatory model has shown itself responsive to market outcomes and public safety concerns. For example, public concerns around edible cannabis goods such as brownies resulted in the governor tightening regulations by instituting limits on product size, THC content (marijuana's main psychoactive ingredient), and ensuring child-proof packaging. In the meantime, more mundane questions of banking regulation are slowly being resolved.

Washington State opted for a more centralized regulatory model and has overseen a bumpier transition. Its experience highlights a core issue in planning for a licit market—taking back control from the illicit one. Its medical marijuana industry was widely viewed as poorly regulated, and much effort has gone into clamping down on it while scaling up the recreational market by creating a number of hard targets, such as the square feet of cannabis plants to be grown (two million) and the number of retail licenses to be allocated (334). Rather than allowing medical businesses to transition into recreational ones, as Colorado has done, the Washington Liquor Control Board aims to build a new system of licensed premises through open bidding. Supply shortfalls, high prices, and a deluge of new applications has delayed the rollout of the system, and the state has struggled to take much business from the black market. Some also attribute the uncompetitive prices to high taxes.

Oregon's legalization initiative, which will likely resemble Washington State's model, has not yet gone into effect. In Washington,

D.C., the local government has moved to a legalized "grow and give" model, in which citizens can legally grow, share, and consume cannabis. This model is meant to avoid commercialization. Meanwhile, in Alaska in February 2015, an initiative became law that allows residents to grow up to six plants and share up to an ounce. The state has given itself one year to develop a regulatory model for commercial retail sales. As *The Economist* reported, the Alaskan case in particular will provide enormous insights to how consumers respond to price drops. Alaska is the furthest U.S. state from Mexico, the source of much of the illegal cannabis in the United States. The extra distance results in extremely high prices—around $2,500–$4,000 wholesale per pound versus border regions where it can be bought for several hundred dollars. If consumption does not increase substantially with the lower prices that will come with legalization, the arguments for continued prohibition elsewhere will become ever more tenuous.

AROUND THE WORLD

The range of approaches to marijuana legalization outside the United States is just as varied. Jamaica is in the midst of a policy reevaluation, beginning with a recent legislative shift toward the decriminalization of consumption and the legalization of personal cultivation of up to five plants. The new law contains provisions for regulating medical and religious uses of the plant, and it remains to be seen whether these provisions will form a mechanism for broader commercialization or state monopolization and, thus, a new source of revenue for the government.

The Netherlands, through non-enforcement of national laws, has a world famous "coffee shop" system to provide de facto legal sales, but supply remains prohibited. According to a 2013 report by the Open Society Foundations Global Drug Policy Program, the result has been the creation of separated illicit drug markets. In other words, there is significant evidence that the Dutch have successfully prevented the interaction between those seeking to consume cannabis and those supplying harder drugs. Where one buys cannabis in the Netherlands is not the same as where one goes to buy cocaine or heroin. One of the stated goals of marijuana prohibition is to forestall the so-called gateway effect, and it seems that the Dutch have actually achieved this outcome by de facto legalization. The Open Society report cites data that "in Sweden, 52 percent of marijuana users report that other drugs are available from their usual cannabis source. In the Netherlands, only 14 percent of marijuana users can get other drugs from their cannabis source." Meanwhile, youth usage rates of cannabis and cocaine are lower in Amsterdam than in the United States and the Dutch cannabis market is estimated to generate $440 million in sales annually.

Spain remains the best case study of gray-market systems for recreational cannabis. Its system relies on so-called Cannabis Social Clubs. As a briefing by Transform Drug Policy Foundation explains, "Cannabis social clubs (CSCs) are private, non-profit organizations in which cannabis is collectively grown and distributed to registered members. With no profit motive to increase cannabis consumption or initiate new users, the clubs offer a more cautious, public health-centered alternative to large-scale retail cannabis markets dominated by commercial enterprises." Although production remains technically illegal, personal cultivation and sharing has been accepted under an expanded definition of decriminalization of consumption. Up to 400 CSCs exist throughout Spain. The government has periodically interfered in their operation and recently started cracking down on them again, likely as a means to prevent their evolution into a coffee shop system akin to that in the Netherlands. Nevertheless, it seems likely these CSCs will persist and represent an alternative model for states in Europe and elsewhere to examine and pursue.

Finally, politicians in countries as diverse as Morocco and Zambia have been warming to the idea of legalized production. As *The Guardian* reported last year, a Green Party candidate in the Zambian presidential election promised to exploit the global undersupply of medical cannabis. Israel, long a pioneer in medical cannabis provision and research, seems unwilling for the moment to step into the void because it would bring unwanted international attention. The Czech Republic, meanwhile, received press attention in 2013 for domestic efforts to secure new sources of supply to bring down the domestic price of its medical cannabis.

The international trend is clear: countries are openly countenancing policies that would have been unthinkable just five or ten years ago. For his part, Kleiman writes that "the places that legalize cannabis first will provide—at some risk to their own populations—an external benefit to the rest of the world in the form of knowledge, however the experiments turn out." So what have the early adopters taught us?

GROWTH OPPORTUNITIES

On balance, it would seem that the gray-area models represent the best alternative to prohibition in areas where they can be made to operate. The Dutch system, despite the continued problems around the prohibition of supply, has been a clear success on many of the metrics upon which policies are judged. The ability of the state to roll back excessive commercialization and shrink the scale of the coffee shop model when it desires is something that would diminish under a fully legalized market, though it would also be harmful to those working in the retail market. Similarly, the Spanish market, despite a general lack of research, appears to offer a strong example for other countries to consider emulating. In the case of the Uruguay model, it remains too early to tell. Nevertheless, the level of state control is encouraging and something that countries that desire to institute fully regulated markets would certainly wish to emulate, depending on how the Uruguay experience plays out.

However, the pragmatic Dutch and Spanish attitudes and the strict supply regulation models may not work or be sustained in the United States, where restrictions on advertising and commercialization would run afoul of the First Amendment guarantees to free speech and an entrepreneurial culture. Further, the inability of the U.S. system to foster pragmatic gray-area accommodations between federal goals and state desires is already apparent in the constant harassment of the medical marijuana sector by federal agents and prosecutors. Although the medical marijuana question has been defused by federal legislation, the recreational question remains particularly poignant given uncertainty over the federal governments' continued acceptance of state-led legalization. Under this situation, a fully legalized market may well be the only long-term solution, and so officials would do well to preempt the downsides of that model with strong national regulations, which can prevent a regulatory race to the bottom among states. This point is well highlighted by Kleiman and his colleagues, who point to the case of interstate tobacco smuggling within the United States as a means to avoid individual state taxes.

Meanwhile, Jonathan Caulkins, a professor of public policy at Carnegie Mellon, warns that legalization of production and market forces could lead to a dangerous price drop and rising consumption. He points to data from the western United States in 2008, where wholesale prices under prohibition were around $3,500 per pound. At the same time, in the highly regulated small-scale medical cannabis production system in the Netherlands, cannabis sold for roughly $490 per pound. He suggests that under a highly commercialized large-scale production model, prices in the United States could decline by 90 percent. Assuming a straightforward interaction between price and demand (a significant assumption), one might expect potentially large increases in consumption under legal regulation.

Others place more faith in the ability of governments to tax and regulate the substance, thereby mitigating the price differential between the licit and illicit markets, and diverting the returns toward government rather than criminal coffers. The evidence from Colorado is clearly encouraging from this perspective. On February 27, the state's Department of Revenue's Marijuana Enforcement Division released its first ever Annual Report. As Christopher Ingraham for *The Washington Post* noted, total statewide cannabis sales hit $700 million in 2014, medical accounting for $386 million and recreational accounting for $313 million. Total tax revenue from the recreational and medical markets was $63 million, plus $13 million in licenses and fees. By 2016, it's expected to be a $1 billion retail market, contributing $94 million in tax revenue annually—likely an understatement of the full economic contribution, as tourism and other retail sales related to cannabis are not counted.

Within Colorado, implementation has varied; twice as many Colorado jurisdictions opted out of allowing either retail or medicinal pot businesses as have permitted them. Yet around 58 percent of Colorado residents remain supportive of legalization, with 38 percent against. Meanwhile, the expected downsides have not emerged. Car accidents are stable and crime has fallen. The long-term consequences, such as the evolution of usage rates, remain to be seen, but it seems reasonable to subscribe to U.S. Attorney General Eric Holder's assessment of being "cautiously optimistic" of the outcomes.

Legalization will also have some impact on producer and transit countries, especially if home-grown marijuana in the United States heavily displaces illicit imports from Mexico. A conservative estimate by RAND in 2010 suggested that 15–26 percent of Mexican drug trafficking organizations' revenue is derived from cannabis. Although losing that business would not deal the groups a death blow, it would severely hurt their operations, including their ability to purchase weapons and bribe police and politicians. Further, farmers will lose the incentive to partake in this illicit market (although potentially seeking other illicit revenue sources). Anecdotal evidence suggests that the bottom may be falling out of the Mexican cannabis cultivation market. As one Mexican pot grower told NPR reporter John Burnett, "Two or three years ago, a kilogram [2.2 pounds] of marijuana was worth $60 to $90 . . . But now they're paying us $30 to $40 a kilo. It's a big difference. If the U.S. continues to legalize pot, they'll run us into the ground."

The challenges ahead are numerous. States will have to effectively regulate cannabis markets to maintain high prices, minimize rises in consumption, and successfully undercut the black market. It is too soon to tell whether legalization will be a boon or a bane, nevertheless, the more regulatory experiments out there, the more researchers will be in a position to build empirically sound arguments for and against types of legalization policies.

Caliphate of Law

ISIS' Ground Rules

Andrew F. March and Mara Revkin

THAIER AL-SUDAN / REUTERS

A wall painted with the black flag commonly used by Islamic State militants in al-Alamm, March 10, 2015.

O
n June 29, 2014, the Islamic State (also called ISIS) declared the "State of the Islamic Caliphate," which adherents and supporters regard as nothing less than a restoration of the

ANDREW F. MARCH is Associate Professor of Political Science at Yale University.

MARA REVKIN is a J.D./Ph.D. student in political science at Yale University and Yale Law School. Follow her on Twitter @MaraRevkin.

earliest model of the caliphate. Banners throughout the lands ruled by ISIS proclaim it the *khilafa 'ala minhaj al-nubuwwa*—or the "caliphate in the prophetic method"—that is, the model set out by Muhammad himself 1,400 years ago.

More remarked on by Western observers, of course, have been ISIS' gruesome public beheadings, mass executions, immolations, and its slave markets and cryptic apocalyptic notions. Its spectacular and seemingly arbitrary violence has spawned an obsession with dramatic questions: Is ISIS truly "Islamic"? Or is it better compared to modern nihilists and exotic apocalyptic death cults?

Although such questions make for interesting thought experiments, they do not bring the world closer to understanding how ISIS governs tens of thousands of square miles and millions of people. Indeed, whatever ISIS believes about the apocalypse, it sees itself as creating a distinctive and authentic legal order for the here and now, one that is based not only on a literal (if selective) reading of early Islamic materials but also on a long-standing theory of statecraft and legal authority.

It isn't surprising that ISIS makes claims derived from Islamic law or that a group controlling territory should enact lawlike structures of governance. After all, states are built on legal institutions that legitimize the regime's monopoly on violence, resource extraction, and political authority. So what is ISIS actually doing and saying on the ground in the areas it controls? Ongoing research shows that ISIS is using Islamic law not simply to terrorize foreign hostages and non-Muslim groups, such as Christians or Yazidis, but also to establish a social contract with the Muslim population it aspires to govern. Despite suggestions that ISIS has "peaked" or is already in "decline," its concern for establishing a law-based political order indicates that the group has aspirations for long-term governance—aspirations that should be taken seriously.

FOUNDING PRINCIPLES

ISIS aims to establish scrupulous legality for itself, from its very "constitutional" foundations to its narrowest public policies. This process, in fact, began up to a year before the declaration of the caliphate in a series of texts laying the groundwork for the future state, and it continues today with administrative guidelines for groups and individuals that wish to pledge allegiance to the caliphate. Allegiance (*bay'a*) documents are frequently published online and reveal a consistency in language and substance.

Here, three points are worth noting. First, these texts aim to prove that Muslims have an unavoidable religious obligation not just to create any ordinary state governed by shariabut to restore the specific office of the caliphate. "Without the condition of the caliphate being realized," ISIS clarified in its official public declaration of the caliphate, "all power is simply worldly kingship, domination and governance, accompanied by destruction, corruption, injustice, coercion and fear, and the degradation and decline of humans to the level of animals. This is the truth of the succession to God, for which God has created us." Second, the group takes pains to justify the legality of Abu Bakr al-Baghdadi's own personal election to the office. The doctrinal basis for this was laid at least a year in advance, for example in the document "*Madd al-ayadi libay'at al-Baghdadi,*" which was released July 22, 2013. That work describes the classical conditions of eligibility for the caliph and then outlines Baghdadi's fulfillment of them. Finally, ISIS leaders appear bent on avoiding some of the problematic features of modern Islamic lawmaking—namely, the ubiquitous tendency to issue codes of law and formal constitutions. Instead, the group has refused to codify any but the most widely known Islamic legal rules in order to avoid the emulation of modern nation-states. For ISIS, God's law can already be found in the primary texts of revelation (with some support from medieval scholars where necessary), and it is the job of worthy judges to enforce it.

Likewise, the caliph is seen as a custodian of divine law. His power is not portrayed as absolute, but he does have plenty of room to issue laws and policies. The system follows a classical Islamic theory of statecraft known as *siyasa shar'iyya*. The term means "religiously legitimate governance," but it implies more than just the application of formal sharia. Instead, it sets up a kind a dualistic

A man purported to be the reclusive leader of ISIS, Abu Bakr al-Baghdadi, July 5, 2014.

model of law and governance. On the one hand, the system requires sharia courts for the application of Islamic legal rules in routine matters for which specific rules exist. But it recognizes that rules do not exist for every conceivable matter. And so the *"siyasa shar'iyya"* theory posits that there are legitimate authorities—from market inspectors to military commanders and governors up to the caliph himself—that have the right to make lawlike decisions as long as those decisions are issued solely with the welfare (*maslaha*) of the Muslim community in mind and do not violate known laws.

Within the framework of this theory, ISIS has established both sharia courts for unexceptional Islamic rulings over civil and some criminal matters and other kinds of courts that deal with military discipline or complaints from the population, including grievances against ISIS fighters (many of whom have actually been punished after such complaints).

LAW AND ORDER

Within the *siyasa shar'iyya* system, ISIS has been able to create rules and regulations to govern civilians, discipline its own fighters, and control territory. Such regulations often deal with matters that were not directly addressed by the revelatory texts (for example, fines for traffic violations). But they are ultimately anchored in an Islamic legal order nonetheless. For evidence, look to four of the most important areas of regulation—citizenship, land, trade, and war.

The ISIS legal system purports to establish a relationship between government and the people that is based on accountability and Islamic justice, according to which the caliph himself can be removed by the Shura council if he fails to fulfill his obligations. The theory of the caliphate implies a law-based social contract with reciprocal obligations and rights between the caliph and the people, whom ISIS calls "subjects" (*ri'aya*, or simply "the Muslims"). The group issues a variety of rules and regulations designed to enforce those subjects' compliance with their obligations. It also guarantees a limited number of legally enforceable rights—for example, the right to file complaints or charges against ISIS combatants or officials. As one propaganda brochure from Raqqa states, "The Islamic State is just and there is no distinction between a soldier and a Muslim [civilian]. In the shariacourts, all are held accountable and no one has immunity." Additionally, ISIS claims that its subjects have the right to equal treatment before the law of God: "The people are as equal as the teeth of a comb. There is no difference the rich and the poor and the strong and the weak. The holder of a right has redress, and the grievance of an injured party will be answered."

Different legal obligations apply to Muslims and non-Muslims. Christians and Jews are allowed to live and work in the caliphate in exchange for paying an annual tax, which in Iraq was recently set at a rate of four gold dinars for the wealthy, two dinars for middle-income, and one dinar for the poor. At the same time, ISIS has also developed legal justifications for the extermination of certain classes of non-Muslim minorities within the caliphate's territory. Prior to the capture of Sinjar in Iraq, ISIS claims, its religious scholars conducted research on the Yazidis to determine whether they should legally be considered an unbelieving group "by origin" (*asli*) or one that was originally Muslim and only later apostatized. Ultimately,

ISIS fighters burn confiscated cigarettes in the city of Raqqa, April 2, 2014.

ISIS determined that the Yazidis were a polytheist group by origin and therefore concludes, "Unlike the Jews and Christians, there was no room for jizyah payment . . . and [the Yazidis] can only be given an ultimatum to repent or face the sword."

Of course, all residents of the caliphate, whether Muslim or non-Muslim, are prohibited from engaging in criminal activity or other forms of misconduct. ISIS publishes specific guidelines for the punishment of crimes that are specifically defined in the Koran (known as "*hadd* crimes"), but it also metes out discretionary punishments ("*ta ʿzir*") for ones that are not. Based on data collected on ISIS courts and policing activities, we have identified three main categories of punishable crimes and misconduct: crimes threatening the state and public order, including espionage, treason, collaborating with foreign interests, embezzlement of public funds; crimes against religion or public morality, including adultery, sodomy, blasphemy, apostasy, pornography, selling or consuming drugs and alcohol, and witchcraft; and crimes or torts against particular individuals, which include theft, burglary, home invasion, rape, armed robbery, and murder.

In addition to rules regulating subjects' behavior, ISIS issues rules designed to expand the population and socialize children with Islamic values. Such regulations include mandatory education through the ninth grade (girls and boys are educated in different schools) and prohibitions on the use of birth control. These rules are generally oriented toward increasing the population of the caliphate and producing obedient subjects who can be easily governed and conscripted as fighters.

In terms of land laws, establishing a legal basis for territorial conquest is important to ISIS for both ideological and practical reasons. First, on an ideological level, ISIS purports to be reclaiming lands that were unlawfully expropriated from Muslims by Crusaders and colonial powers. It needs a legal foundation to justify those claims.

Second, on a practical level, ISIS is attempting to establish territorial control under conditions of war in which land rights are at best uncertain and at worst a subject of violent conflict. It is impossible to govern such contested territory without a legitimate claim to sovereignty and rules for property ownership and land use.

Accordingly, ISIS has articulated elaborate rules for property and land. For example, it has laws for the seizure of war booty, stating that jihadists should take only what is necessary to advance the objectives of jihad. ISIS has also issued a fatwa justifying the expropriation of agricultural businesses that previously belonged to apostates before the group captured them, and additional regulations for the distribution of such confiscated property as charity for the poor and to recruits. One propaganda magazine illustrates the importance of property as an incentive for recruitment: "Do not worry about money or accommodations for yourself and your family. There are plenty of homes and resources to cover you and your family." Meanwhile, ISIS has also attempted to regulate agriculture and environmental protection. For example, a recent announcement from Deir ez-Zor in Syria prohibits fishermen from using electrical current, poison, or dynamite to kill fish, out of concern that such methods cause congenital defects in minnows and are also detrimental to the health of human consumers.

In terms of trade law, ISIS makes clear that the preferred vocation for subjects is jihad and that it frowns on peaceful alternatives such as farming. Propaganda advises Muslims to earn a living "by performing jihād and then taking from the agriculture of his kāfir enemies, not by dedicating his life to agriculture like his enemies do." However, in recognition of the reality that the caliphate's economy will rely on other forms of productive work, the group has developed rules to regulate labor and commerce. It requires fighters who "abandon jihad and work to improve their wealth and land" to pay taxes that will further the fight. Taxation is thus a justification for otherwise impermissible forms of commerce, and it also serves to reinforce the concept of a social contract in which residents of the caliphate perform obligations in exchange for assurances of accountable government and legally enforceable rights. In some places, the group taxes at a rate of 2.5 percent on real estate, clothing, food, vehicles, and more. In addition, ISIS sets prices for housing rents, medications sold at pharmacies, and childbirth operations performed in its hospitals, and has even issued a fatwa requiring that the price of counterfeit goods be lower than the price of the authentic product.

Finally, there are the rules related to war. Here, ISIS claims to follow Islamic laws of armed conflict. And, according to ISIS propaganda, the caliph is personally obligated to ensure combatants' compliance with them: "The leader is required to ensure that he and his soldiers are held responsible for the rights that Allah has made obligatory and the limits that He has set." ISIS has published guidelines, either as official fatwas or legal opinions authored by ISIS-affiliated clerics, specifying the conditions under which enemy combatants may be targeted, tortured, mutilated, or killed as well as rules governing the ransom of non-Muslim hostages. So ISIS can claim that its combatants are acting lawfully according to the group's own rules, even though the United Nations has reported that "ISIS is violating binding international humanitarian law." ISIS also has laws for the provision of security guarantees, called "*aman* documents," for journalists and humanitarian workers seeking access to ISIS-controlled areas. Rules for the treatment of prisoners and slaves do include certain limitations, such as a prohibition on separating a mother from her young children, but they also permit sexual slavery as a legally permissible alternative to adultery. ISIS also regulates and censors fighters' communication through, for example, a decree that prohibits combatants from publishing photographs of enemies killed in battle and a ban on using Apple products and other GPS-enabled devices that, ISIS leaders worry, the U.S.-led coalition could use to help target airstrikes.

COURT ORDER

ISIS enforces its rules and regulations through its internal security sector and two separate police units. One of the police forces, called the "Islamic police," is responsible for ordinary law enforcement and public safety. Its responsibilities include conducting inspections at checkpoints and issuing tickets for traffic violations. According to

U.S. DEPARTMENT OF DEFENSE / REUTERS

Pictures showing an ISIS Command and Control Center in Syria before and after it was struck by bombs dropped by a U.S. F-22 fighter jet, September 23, 2014.

ISIS propaganda, this force contains legal specialists who report to a senior jurist, who in turn serves as a direct link to judges in the courts. When dealing with interpersonal disputes, such jurists will first attempt to resolve the conflict through informal mediation. But if mediation fails, the jurist can refer the dispute to an ISIS court.

The second police force is a religious morals unit called the "*hisba.*" The mandate of this body is to "promote virtue and prevent vice to dry up sources of evil, prevent the manifestation of disobedience, and urge Muslims toward well-being." Activities include enforcing the prohibition on commercial activity during prayer time, responding to reports of drug or alcohol use, and destroying banned materials (including musical instruments, cigarettes, or polytheistic idols). The religious police are also responsible for investigating alleged violations of sharia and may refer more serious crimes to courts.

ISIS has established official courts in Syria, Iraq, and Libya, and proto-courts are reportedly operating in the recently annexed Sinai province as well as border areas of Lebanon. Although ISIS claims to control territory in parts of Algeria and Nigeria through its annexation of other jihadist groups (Jund al-Khilafah and Boko Haram) that have pledged allegiance, courts have not been established in these areas—yet. But as ISIS begins to communicate instructions and guidance to its distant franchises, these groups may come under pressure to establish the kinds of legal and judicial institutions that characterize ISIS governance in Syria and Iraq.

In general, the ISIS judiciary is organized into three main branches: a division for complaints (*mazalim*), including grievances against ISIS public officials and combatants; Islamic courts, including the Supreme Islamic Court located in Mosul, which deals with violations of ISIS laws and government matters; and the Diwan al-Hisba, which adjudicates crimes or misconduct referred by the morality police.

ISIS regulates its judiciary through a top-down bureaucratic chain that starts with the Sharia Council, which is headed by Baghdadi himself. Under the authority of the Sharia Council, each *wali* (the governor of a regional administrative division called a *wilaya*) oversees a shariadeputy who in turn supervises the *wilaya*-level sha-riacommission. The shariacommissions (*hay'at al-shari'a*) are responsible for overseeing courts and the work of judges. ISIS disciplines and even executes its own judges when they refuse to support the caliphate's official position on legal questions. For example, one judge was removed from his post and is expected to face trial for voicing opposition to the legal ruling justifying the immolation of a Jordanian pilot. Another ISIS judge was "disappeared" in Deir ez-Zor after he objected to the torture of prisoners in ISIS jails. Still others have been executed on charges of treason and collaborating with foreign governments.

In addition to punishing its own judges, ISIS has executed independent jurists when they issue unauthorized fatwas that are deemed too radical. For example, in one case, ISIS executed one such jurist after convicting him of spreading *fitna* (strife or discord) by advocating excessive "takfīr" of other Muslim jihadists (*takfir*, in Islamic law, is the practice of declaring someone to be an apostate and therefore a legitimate target for killing).

ISIS operates numerous prisons in connection with its court system. Although precise statistics are not available, Amnesty International reported in December 2013 that ISIS was operating at least seven detention facilities in Raqqa and Aleppo provinces alone. One of the functions of these prisons is to rehabilitate criminals for eventual reintegration into society; ISIS employs clerics in prisons to visit with and educate the inmates. Although the organization claims to guarantee certain rights for detainees, including a pretrial detention limit of seven days before the accused person is entitled to a court hearing, reports of arbitrary arrests and torture in prisons are widespread, and in some ISIS-controlled areas, civilians have staged protests to demand the release of detainees.

LAWFARE

It is too early to tell how long the caliphate will last, but its radicalism—the group's effort to base its authority on what it thinks is the "prophetic method"—seems more easy to sustain in times of war and emergency. In peacetime, ISIS would have only two paths: first (and more likely), it could move toward the increasingly arbitrary corrupt rule of warlords governing an impoverished and enclosed territory; and second, it could become an increasingly "normal" state, in which the simplicity of rules and institutions plucked out of early Islamic history gives way to bureaucratic administration and positive law.

For now, ISIS' ideas have filled a hole both in governance in Iraq and Syria and in the global Salafi-jihadist political imagination. In the long run, the ISIS legacy will be not only its gruesome record of sadistic violence but also its profound challenge to existing Islamist thinking. It is a rebuttal to the long-standing Islamist view that modern, centralized states can be "Islamized" within their existing institutions merely by substituting codified positive laws with codified "Islamic" laws. It also contravenes the al Qaeda–style strategy of spectacular violence directed at Western and Muslim targets without long-term governance of territory in which Muslims are the majority. It would not be surprising if ISIS' legal strategy enhances its own global prestige at the expense of al Qaeda and gives inspiration to groups seeking to govern immediately over whatever territories they manage to seize by establishing sharia courts, *hisba* patrols, and military and administrative courts. Authority in these territories can be ratified after the fact as "delegated" from the caliph in Mosul. In the end, victory in the jihadist imagination will look less and less like the glorious toppling of dictators in national capitals such as Amman, Cairo, and Rabat, and more and more like the declaration of liberated *wilayat* until those isolated patches are woven into a single mantle covering the entire *ummah*.

The Balkans, Interrupted

The Protests in Macedonia are Only the Beginning

Edward P. Joseph

Visitors walk on an art installation inside a bunker near Konjic, Bosnia and Herzegovina, April 24, 2015.

L ike most terrorists, he was young. He had been born in the days just before bitter hatred engulfed his country; not long after his birth, his father had been seized by authorities and

EDWARD P. JOSEPH is Executive Director of the Institute of Current World Affairs and a lecturer at Johns Hopkins School of Advanced International Studies.

killed, along with scores of other Sunni Muslims. Two weeks ago, the 24-year-old son marched into a police station reportedly shouting the jihadist war cry "Allahu Akbar!" and then opened fire, killing one officer and wounding two others, before he was killed in a firefight with police.

Over the weekend, 350 miles to the south, eight more policemen were killed along with 14 suspected terrorists in a raging gunbattle near an international border created in the aftermath of World War I that radicals no longer recognize.

Another day in Syria or Iraq? No, this happened in Europe, an easy day's drive from Vienna. The first attack, in Zvornik, a town in Bosnia's Serb entity, was a shocking reminder of the potential influence of radical Islam in the region, especially in the wake of the rise of the Islamic State (also called ISIS). Only a small number of Bosnians have been radicalized, and even fewer have gone to fight in Syria and Iraq. But in the still-fractured Balkans, it doesn't take many radicals to destabilize a country.

Nor is radical Islam the only threat to years of work and billions in investment in the region by Washington and its European partners. In the wake of the standoff with the West over Ukraine, Russia has stepped up its own role there, with incendiary appeals to Orthodox Slav solidarity. Indeed, Moscow has voiced staunch support for the embattled government in Macedonia, where the second shocking incident occurred. The weekend's firefight, replete with grenades, snipers, and automatic weapons, took place in the town of Kumanovo near the border of Macedonia, Serbia, and Kosovo. The government described the fight as a battle between the police and "one of the most dangerous terrorist groups in the Balkans," presumably meaning Albanian radicals. The real circumstances of the shoot-out are murky and the timing suspicious, coming as the government contends with growing waves of protests over revelations of alleged massive government abuse. As the Macedonian president rushed back from Moscow, his hosts there sharply criticized demonstrators and warned against another "color revolution."

LASZLO BALOGH / REUTERS

A group of Kosovars walk along a road after they crossed the Hungarian-Serbian border near the village of Asotthalom February 6, 2015. The EU is experiencing a steep rise in the number of Kosovo citizens smuggling themselves into the bloc, with 10,000 filing for asylum in Hungary in just one month this year compared to 6,000 for the whole of 2013.

With Macedonia facing potential implosion, with Bosnian unity at its most tenuous since the war, and with Kosovo witnessing a mass exodus of citizens who have given up on its corrupt, divisive government, the three most vulnerable countries of the region stand on a precipice. A slide toward radicalism and inter- or even intraethnic strife, abetted by Russian or Islamist opportunism, is fully plausible. And if it happens, U.S. and European diplomats will be forced to finally answer a question: Who lost the Balkans?

Just as at the height of the wars in former Yugoslavia, Washington and Brussels will likely point fingers at each other. In fact, the blame will be shared. Neither the crises in Ukraine nor those in the Middle East are alibis for the West's timid policies and sporadic attention in recent years. The truth is that although destabilization in the Balkans poses far less of a threat to Western interests than Putin's aggression or ISIS' barbarism, it is a far less difficult challenge to overcome.

There are no nuclear weapons in the region. Suicide terrorism, so far, is extremely rare. And most of all, unlike either Ukraine or the countries of the Middle East, even the most divided countries of southeast Europe still share a common strategic orientation, with generally high rates of support for joining NATO and the EU.

But instead of seizing on this strong foundation to overcome remaining obstacles to Euro-Atlantic integration, the West has allowed the fledgling countries of the region to backslide. Washington prematurely handed over lead responsibility for the Balkans to the EU, which prematurely handed over lead responsibility to the region's leaders. With no meaningful EU carrots or sticks to restrain their behavior, politicians have largely consolidated their corrupt patronage networks, co-opted or intimidated the media, and resisted meaningful reform.

MELEE IN MACEDONIA

Macedonia is a prime example of the consequences of sporadic attention. With intensive international help following the outbreak of hostilities between ethnic Macedonians and Albanians in 2001, the country made steady progress in building joint democratic institutions. In 2006, current Prime Minister Nikola Gruevski took office. After four increasingly dubious elections, he has managed to consolidate power by debilitating the judiciary, marginalizing the opposition, and eviscerating independent media. In 2007, Macedonia ranked number 36, ahead of the United States, in Freedom House's Press Freedom Index. Last year, Macedonia sunk to 123, languishing with the likes of Venezuela. The country's economy, meanwhile, remains afloat through a sharp and unsustainable rise in borrowing.

Still among the region's youngest leaders, Gruevski would be sitting pretty with years left in power were it not for a wiretapping scandal that has revealed the breathtaking extent of government abuse. Released periodically by the opposition, recorded phone calls allegedly describe the government's direct orchestration of financial and electoral fraud, mass electronic surveillance, framing of political opponents for crimes, and even murder. In the most shocking

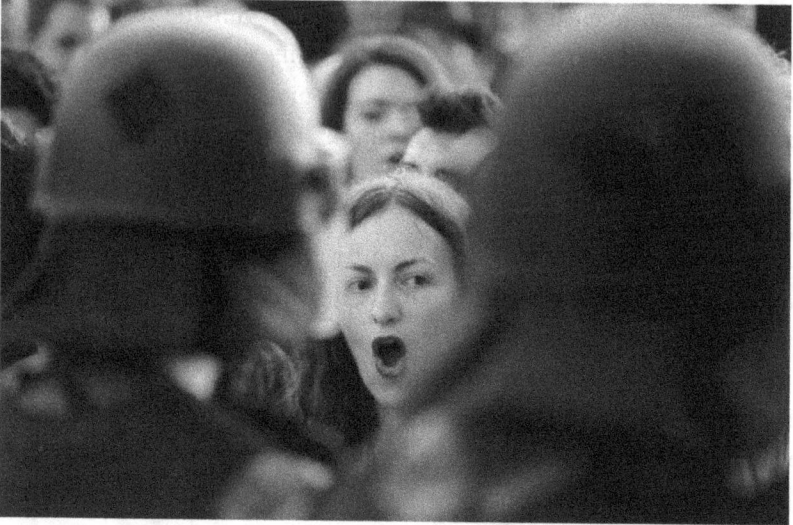

OGNEN TEOFILOVSKI / REUTERS

A girl shouts anti-government slogans in front of the Archaeological Museum in Skopje, Macedonia May 7, 2015. Several hundred people demanded the resignation of Prime Minister Nikola Gruevski.

revelation, released last week, senior government officials are allegedly heard scheming to cover up a dubious car accident that took the life of a noted government critic. Another recording seems to implicate the government in sweeping under the rug a case in which police had beaten a young reveler to death. Gruevski and other government officials have denied the allegations, claiming that the wiretaps are the work of unspecified "foreign agents" who aim to destabilize the country.

In response, this month, thousands of young Macedonians have braved truncheon-bearing riot police to protest. They and the opposition demand that the prime minister and his associates hand power over to a caretaker government that will organize fresh elections while independent investigations into the revelations proceed. With tensions mounting, the opposition has called for a massive demonstration next week. Facing severe legal and personal consequences if he and his cohorts resign, Gruevski appears poised to fight it out to the end, leaving Macedonia's stability in the breach.

The ramifications of the weekend's shocking violence in Kumanovo are as unpredictable as the circumstances of the clash are mysterious. There is precedent in Macedonia for dubious shoot-outs with purported terrorists, including in 2002 when seven migrants from Pakistan and India were shot dead by police in a highly suspicious incident. A Macedonian court eventually cleared the former interior minister of charges of responsibility for the killings. Last month, a Macedonian police spokesman claimed that 40 Albanian radicals attacked a police outpost on the border with Kosovo, yet neither NATO nor the Kosovo police could confirm any such activity.

Ironically, the shoot out between Macedonian police and purported Albanian radicals comes as inter-ethnic relations in the country have made impressive strides. For the first time in its 24-year history as a modern independent state, ethnic Albanians and Macedonians seem largely united in the struggle against perceived dictatorship. With nearly all television stations under the government's grip, it is Alsat, an Albanian-owned station, that is airing the wiretaps and offering extensive airtime to opposition voices, a remarkable gesture of solidarity. Albanian web-sites have published sharp anti-government commentary by ethnic Macedonians, something that was largely unheard of in the traditionally ethnically segregated media sector. The broadcasts have become increasingly awkward for both the ruling and opposition Albanian political parties, which have been curiously silent in the face of the massive scandal.

The international community could play a decisive role in bringing things to a peaceful resolution, but so far its reaction has been tentative. Only the German ambassador has openly called for the government to resign. In the wake of the recent violence, the U.S. embassy joined the EU, NATO, and the Organization for Security and Cooperation in Europe to call, improbably, for "the country's leaders to pull together and engage in dialogue on all issues facing the country."

It is typical of the West to seek to avoid a confrontation with Gruevski, allowing him and other figures to keep the region's open questions simmering. But the one over-arching lesson since the violent collapse of Yugoslavia 25 years ago is that the failure to deal with core problems head-on has only made them harder to resolve in the end. This is especially true in Macdonia's case, where Greece's longstanding objections to the country's name, which Athens sees as theft of Greek heritage, have kept Macedonia out of both NATO (where its membership is on offer) and the EU (with which it is poised to open negotiations). The country's current instability could have been avoided had Skopje been allowed to proceed towards NATO and EU membership. Rather than move toward autocracy, Gruevski would have been constrained by strict requirements that have proved to empower democratic institutions elsewhere.

Rather than forge a trans-Atlantic consensus on the urgency for a compromise on the name—for which many possibilities exist—Washington has focused on the matter only when pressed to do so. In 1995, on the eve of the talks in Dayton, Ohio aimed at ending the war in Bosnia, Richard Holbrooke achieved a modus vivendi between Athens and Skopje. In 2004, crisis in Macedonia prompted the Bush administration to finally recognize Macedonia by its constitutional name. Feared blowback from Greece over this move never materialized. Despite that fact, Washington dropped the issue until the run-up to NATO's 2008 summit, when it was too late to push the parties into compromise. Underscoring the West's impotence on the issue, the International Court of Justice ruled in 2011 that Athens had no right to deny Macedonia entry into NATO. Nonetheless, the alliance continues to leave Skopje, which has fulfilled all requirements for membership, in the waiting room.

Grueski has seized on international paralysis over the name issue to provoke Greece with tacky appeals to Macedonian nationalism. Most recently, he claimed that the wiretaps are part of an international conspiracy designed to force him to jettison the country's name. For its part, Athens has recently emerged as a key player in trans-Atlantic attempts to thwart a planned Russian-Turkish gas pipeline, which boosts the ability of the nearly bankrupt country to stand up to Western pressure on the name issue. In short, as in other cases from the region, Western inattention has only made the question of Macedonia's name more acute and more fraught.

BROKEN BOSNIA

If Macedonia is in acute pain, Bosnia is facing deeper and nearly irreparable injury. Radical Islam and Russian influence are exacerbating ever-present ethnic suspicions. Meanwhile, some of the country's politicians are taking concrete steps to split the country. Ruling Serb and Croat parties recently announced their commitment to thinly veiled separatist agendas. The Republika Srpska parliament even passed a resolution for a separatist referendum that, for the first time, included a concrete date, 2018, for the incendiary plebiscite. If held, the Serb referendum is guaranteed to reopen hostilities.

Bosnia will face near-term tests of its cohesion this summer. In June, long-delayed census results are set to be released, potentially fueling anger among Bosniaks (Bosnian Muslims), Croats, and Serbs alike, each of whom can spin figures to claim advantage or complain of systematic disadvantage. Then, in July, Bosnia will mark the emotional 20th anniversary of the massacre at Srebrenica, where more than 7,000 Bosniak men and boys were killed at the hands of Serb forces.

U.S. and EU leaders have given up on the priority of getting Bosnia to change its outmoded constitution that is responsible for most of the gridlock that keeps the country mired. EU leaders have now coalesced around a new policy of seemingly easier-to-achieve economic and social measures. Next month, the EU and the International Monetary Fund (IMF) are to announce a ballyhooed "reform action plan" meant to spur long overdue cuts to the bloated bureaucracy and other reforms needed for EU accession. Unfortunately, the public is adamantly against cutting public sector jobs, and many politicians rightly fear that reform will force them to privatize public companies they currently manipulate for patronage and graft. Sensing this resistance, and congenitally afraid of confronting local

DADO RUVIC / REUTERS

Bosnian Muslims speak with census surveyer Elvis Spijudic near Srebrenica, October 1, 2013. This was Bosnia's first census as an independent state.

officials, international players are likely to temper their demands for reform. Brussels already fudged its own requirements for the formal association agreement between Bosnia and the EU enacted this year, and officials have made it clear that according Bosnia candidate status is the crux of their latest strategy for the troubled country.

Emphasizing form over substance, the EU is no more likely to achieve desperately needed progress now than it has been over the past nine years. As in Macedonia, it was in 2006 that the democratization process, which had seen fledgling joint institutions take shape under vigorous international stewardship, began to unravel. Prematurely applying a rigid form of local ownership over institutions, recalcitrant officials (particularly in the Serb entity) began to unwind progress and openly challenge the country's unity. As Washington periodically attempted to goad the EU into action and local officials into compromise, Bosnian leaders shrugged off the efforts and the country slumped more deeply into stagnation. With 14 separate governments, the country's institutions today are a dysfunctional relic of the war years, inhibiting investment and interethnic cooperation.

The only positive from the terrorist attack in Zvornik is that it may finally shock international officials into action. An EU-IMF package that links ambitious standards with generous financial incentives and credible penalties—such as visa bans and exposure of financial chicanery for recalcitrant leaders—can finally concentrate minds in Bosnia.

THE KOSOVO EXAMPLE

Concerted effort can also achieve results in Kosovo, the site of the EU's most significant breakthrough. Under Brussels' leadership, and with strong U.S. support, Serbia and Kosovo agreed to normalize their relations two years ago. But bickering between Belgrade and Pristina, abetted by the refusal of five EU countries to recognize independent Kosovo, along with endemic corruption, has left Kosovo in miserable shape. Tens of thousands of Kosovars have left

HAZIR REKA / REUTERS

Potted plants are put in place by local Serbs to form a barricade on the main bridge in the ethnically divided Kosovo town of Mitrovica, June 18, 2014.

the country for the EU, expressing their abject lack of confidence in the future with their feet.

Radical options for unifying Kosovo with Albania, which would reopen conflict with Serbs, continue to find favor. Once exemplary moderates have been hardening their stance against the Brussels-backed compromise. At the same time, Kosovo has seen disturbing signs of Islamist radicals who strike fear in the hearts of Serbs and moderate Albanian Muslims alike. The great worry is that Islamists will find common cause with radical Albanian nationalists, injecting greater instability into a country whose security is still overseen by NATO, along with a substantial EU presence.

Brussels and Washington need to press Albanian leaders to move forward now on key rule of law reforms, while dragging Belgrade and Pristina to agreement on issues arguably far less onerous than those they overcame in 2013. Those talks proved that when Brussels conditions progress toward EU membership on progress in their relations, then Serbs and Albanians begin to move toward compromise.

Dangers abound, but the Balkans are by no means hopeless. The irony of today's crises in Macedonia, Bosnia, and Kosovo is that while some leaders play the nationalism card, more ordinary citizens than ever before are willing to move past ethnic differences. Enough time has been frittered away protracting the region's outstanding issues with abortive, inadequate initiatives. There is no need to squander, through neglect and timidity, a principled (and largely successful) effort begun with courage and vision. More than anything, resolving the region's problems today simply requires that officials once more take them seriously.

When a Bride-to-Be Is a Bride to Buy

In India, a Shortage of Women Generates Demand for Trafficked Brides

Ira Trivedi

A paro from Bihar in Mewat, Haryana. She is not sure how many times she has been sold, March 14, 2014.

IRA TRIVEDI is a New Delhi based journalist and author. Her latest book is *India in Love: Marriage and Sexuality in the Twenty-First Century*.

Nuh, a sleepy, sepia-toned town is a two-hour drive from New Delhi and borders the new-age city of Gurgaon, which sports swanky skyscrapers, luxury residential townships, and gargantuan malls. Nuh, too, is fast transforming from rural to urban: Shopping complexes and car showrooms have sprouted up next to mud huts and maize fields. And yet, that economic growth has not translated into much social change—Nuh is still very backward.

It is in Nuh that I met Shilpa, 30. (Her name has been changed to protect her identity.) She is introduced to me as "molki," a derogatory term that translates from Hindi as "purchased." When Shilpa was 16, her parents entrusted her to a relative who promised to arrange her marriage. He turned out to be a broker in the bride trafficking business and secretly sold her for around 7,500 rupees ($120) to a man in Nuh, in Haryana state. There, Shilpa was treated no better than a slave: Confined to the house so that she wouldn't draw too much attention,

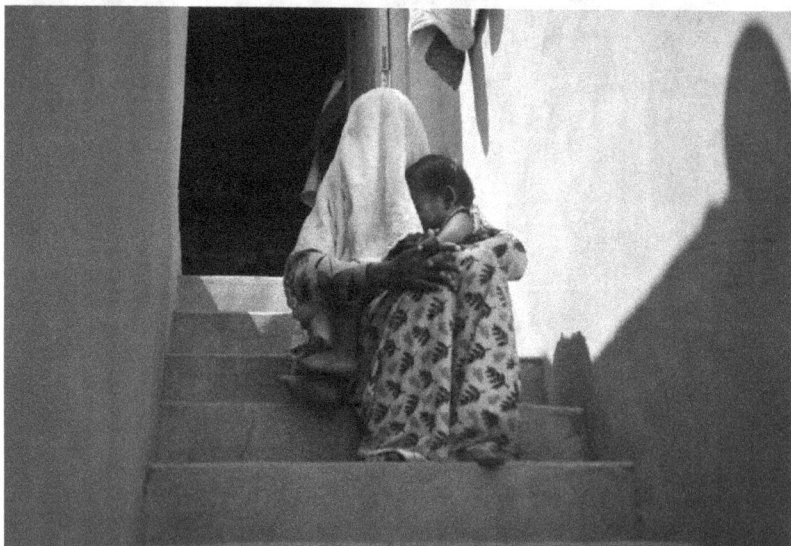

SUBRATA BISWAS / HINDUSTAN TIMES

A bride trafficking survivor, Razia (name changed), sits with her child. She hails from Bhagalpur in Bihar and is not sure how many times she has been sold. She now lives in Mewat, Haryana, March 14, 2014

she cooked for his family, took care of his ailing parents, was "shared" among male relatives, bore her husband four children, and then when he died in a car accident five years ago, was kicked out of her home along with her children. She was left without any savings.

It is not clear how many *paros* (stolen brides) there are in Nuh, but over 9,000 married women out of 10,000 surveyed households in Haryana were purchased from other states, according to a field study conducted by the NGO Drishti Stree Adhyayan Prabodhan Kendra. A 2013 UN report found that the demand for girls of a marriageable age (legally, 18, but nearly 50 percent are married before then) is so high that bride trafficking has turned into a thriving business. According to Shafiq Ur Rehman, the founder of Empower People, an NGO working with survivors of bride trafficking like Shilpa, most of the demand for brides comes from the northwestern states of Haryana, Punjab, Western Uttar Pradesh, Rajasthan, and Gujarat. A deep-set culture of patriarchy, mixed with a high gender imbalance and increasing dowry demands, make bride trafficking endemic to this region.

THE EXCHANGE

I could tell from the moment I met Shilpa that she was an outsider in Nuh. Her Bengali features and accent were both giveaways. She is from Achuri, a small village in West Bengal, nearly one thousand miles east from Haryana, and one of the key states supplying the brides. In that region, a number of factors push families into selling their daughters (most often unintentionally). The first is abject poverty. Livelihoods often depend on agricultural yields, which in turn, rely on the monsoon rains. But precipitation has grown increasingly unpredictable with climate change. At times, the fields flood, wiping out homes and a life's worth of possessions. At others, the sky stays dry all season, and crops wither.

The women, themselves, often do not realize they are being sold, but once they do, it is too late to turn back.

In Achuri, Shilpa's father worked on a farm and owned a little piece of land. Based on Shilpa's stories, their life seems to be fairly standard: working hard to achieve the basics—putting a roof over their heads and food on the table (though no table in this case). When Shilpa was young, they didn't own a television, though today they do, and they all have cellphones. It seemed that the family was remarkable only in one way—that they had five daughters, and no sons.

As the youngest daughter, Shilpa was considered a burden on the family. She had one asset, though, that set her apart from her siblings: her fair skin. That highly desirable trait in India made her a hot commodity and her uncle (her father's youngest brother) whom she referred to as "Chachaji," told her parents that he would take their daughter to Haryana to marry and "settle" her. Shilpa's parents were relieved by the arrangement because it meant that they no longer had to scrounge for a dowry. Without one, Shilpa would have been difficult to marry off, and her parents would have had to bear the stigma of keeping an unmarried daughter at home. The uncle even "gifted" them 2,500 rupees ($40), which the parents thought was simply an act of largesse.

On the day of the exchange, Shilpa embarked on a 24-hour train ride from Achuri to Nuh, accompanied by Chachaji. She remembers feeling mostly confused and scared, but had seen women throughout her childhood leaving Achuri to get married, so she assumed that her journey was nothing out of the ordinary. When she arrived in Nuh, she met her intended husband for the first time. He was 20 years her senior.

"Were you unhappy?" I asked her. "No not really," she replied. For a decade, she thought that her cloistered existence was what married life was meant to be like. But she had accepted her fate then, as she has now.

Bride brokers often masquerade as matchmakers, which traditionally request a fee to arrange a marriage. So it is a relief for families when they receive money in return for their daughters instead of having to pay for services, but most do not realize their daughter is being sold into the bride trade. Even today, Shilpa's parents do not seem to have a full understanding of what happened

A bride trafficking survivor sits in the corner of a room of a house in Mewat, Haryana. Paros don't get much respect, March 13, 2014.

so many years ago. Chachaji had told Shilpa's parents that the family in Nuh were his relatives. Shilpa's parents definitely did not know that he was in the business of buying and selling brides.

The women, themselves, often do not realize they are being sold, but once they do, it is too late to turn back. Traffickers avoid getting caught because girls like Shilpa, who are far from home and lack social support, rarely lodge complaints about any mistreatment and do not trust the police.

What makes this all so shocking is that, even as India is developing at an astounding rate, the sale of women into marriage is only growing more common. The number of trafficked women is growing by 20 percent every year. This rise in trafficking is directly caused by an acute gender imbalance in India, but the skew is felt most deeply in northwestern states, which are also rigidly conservative, ruled by the *khap panchayat* or unelected, usually all-male councils that often operate above the law and enforce traditional marriage and caste rules. They have banned cross-caste, as well as

SUBRATA BISWAS / HINDUSTAN TIMES

A bride trafficking survivor, Razia (name changed), lives with her children in a dilapidated hut in Mewat, Haryana. Razia's husband tried to sell her when she was pregnant with their second child, March 15, 2014.

inter-clan or village marriages. (In some places in India, marriages between blood relations and between those of the same social rank and geography are all considered incest.) *Khaps* may forbid a man and a woman in the same *gotra*, or subsect of a caste, from marrying. These rules further reduce the pool of available women that men can marry. The *khaps* have begun to relax these stringent rules around marriage, however, after realizing how much they have exacerbated the bride shortage.

Khaps also set cultural norms and values and often permit honor killings, which perpetuate the devaluation of women that underpins bride trafficking. The *khaps* first came to international attention in 2012 after a group in Haryana blamed young girls' libidos for inciting a string of rapes across the state. They proposed marrying girls at a younger age to ensure their "sexual appetites" were satisfied within the bounds of marriage. One *khap* told the *New York Times* at that time, "Women maintain a family's honor. Not men. If she cannot keep her honor, it is solely her fault." With the rise in sexual violence toward women, families seek to marry girls off as soon as possible to "preserve their honor." They feel that keeping unmarried girls at home increase their chances of being violated and bringing shame upon the family. Somehow, it is thought that when a woman is married, she is less prone to danger. This is of course, not true. But it may be yet another factor that fuels bride trafficking.

NO MODERATION IN MODERNIZATION

When harsh cultural practices meet modern technology, the combination can be lethal. Although India has always been patriarchal, the sharp decline in the sex ratio did not occur until the 1990s with the large-scale availability of a machine intended, of all things, to protect maternal and infant health: the ultrasound. Instead of simply saving lives, its use in India led to a surge in the abortion of female fetuses. Since 1991, 80 percent of India's districts have recorded a declining sex ratio with the state of Punjab being

SUBRATA BISWAS / HINDUSTAN TIMES

Rubina (name changed) was 15 years old when a middleman brought her from Assam. She is now living in deplorable conditions in Mewat, Haryana, March 15, 2014.

the worst, followed by Haryana, Maharashtra, Gujarat, and Himachal Pradesh. Ever year, 500,000 girls are lost to female feticide. An estimated four to 12 million selective abortions of girls have occurred in India in the past three decades, and the massacre has not stopped.

Haryana, where Shilpa was sold, has one of the country's most skewed sex ratios at 879 men per 1,000 women (the national average is 927 to 1,000, according to the 2011 census). The sex ratio of children under six is worse: 834 girls to 1,000 boys (the national figure is 914 to 1,000). That means in India's youngest age group, there are 40 million more males than females.

Poorer, rural communities, like Shilpa's hometown, however, may have limited access to ultrasounds and as a result, exhibit a much more balanced gender ratio. In West Bengal, there are 934 males to 1,000 females. And so they are prime territory for bride traffickers, who target the poorest villages in India, usually in Jharkhand, Bihar, Assam, and West Bengal.

Modernization has been unkind to India's women in yet another way. The speed of economic growth in India is creating a desperate type of consumption that fuels both the demand and the supply side of bride trafficking: weddings and dowries. India's wedding industry is worth an estimated $25.5 billion with an annual growth rate of 20 to 25 percent. The average middle-class family spends more than $12,158 on a wedding, nearly double the median income of an average middle-class family, which was $625 between 2011 and 2012.

To many, the birth of a daughter signifies a large, crippling expense, one that can be avoided if a female fetus is either aborted or a daughter is handed off to a bride trafficker.

In a sense, the dowry, banned in 1961 after an escalation of dowry-related death and violence, has been replaced by a lavish wedding. The extravagance is not only normal nowadays but necessary. It is considered to be a display of a family's prosperity and wealth. For some families, failing to provide an elaborate wedding can lead to dishonor or even death.

I recently visited a courthouse in New Delhi where four sets of parents waited their turn to make their case before a judge for the murder of their daughters over unmet wedding or dowry demands. I spoke to one family, the Sharmas, who told me that their daughter Priyanka was poisoned after they had failed deliver a car promised to her husband's family.

"They wanted a grand wedding," said the father. "But we could not afford it, so we told them that we would give them a car instead. When we went to buy the car, [the dealers] told us that we would have to sell our farmland, which is our only means of survival. When we couldn't give them the car immediately, [the husband's family] killed our daughter. Our daughter alone was not enough for them."

What happened to Priyanka is, tragically, not uncommon. According to the National Crime Records Bureau, a total of 91,200 dowry deaths were reported in the country between January 1, 2001 and December 31, 2012.

SUBRATA BISWAS / HINDUSTAN TIMES

Sayedan (name changed) was trafficked at the age of 12 from Bangladesh by a local man in Mewat, Haryana, March 15, 2014.

That is why to many, the birth of a daughter signifies a large, crippling expense, one that can be avoided if a female fetus is either aborted or a daughter is handed off to a bride trafficker.

A SOCIAL DISASTER

With excess males comes excess patriarchy. According to Harvard psychologist Robert Epstein, who has collected data from more than a hundred countries, including the United States, in a male-dominated society, more women are forced out of the workforce either by choice or force. "Extra males affect the social system quite dramatically," Epstein told me. "Even now, there are women being drugged and kidnapped from Bangladesh and poor Indian states because there is a shortage of young females. Take that effect and magnify it over a period of years. It's a social disaster."

The solution cannot be merely an economic one. Studies by Yale Economist Nancy Qian in China show that increasing household income alone has no effect on sex ratios. Increasing male income (holding female income constant) decreases educational levels and survival rates for girls, but has no effect on boys' educational attainment. In contrast, increasing female income (holding male income constant) increases survival rates for girls. Moreover, increasing the mother's income increases education for all children.

Even without such data, the women of India seem to understand that if they want to change the status quo, they have to do it themselves. In Haryana, for example, more women have been protesting against sexual violence, harassment, dowry deaths, and female feticide. Last December, two sisters attending college in Rohtak, Haryana, a two-hour drive from Nuh, rose to national fame when they beat up three men who tried molesting them on a public bus. NGOs like Empower People are helping women like Shilpa realize their rights.

Since Shilpa was ousted from her husband's home, she has worked as a maid in Nuh. And it is only recently that she began speaking up about her experiences as a *paro*. She does not provide her real name, fearing that her in-laws may find her, abuse her, and extort her for money. Though Shilpa lives hand-to-mouth, often making only enough to provide shelter and basic sustenance for herself and her children, she is happier than when she lived with her husband and his family. She tells me with a smile that for the first time in her life she feels free.

As the number of educated women and those in organized workforces increases—today, those numbers are at their highest (although India continues to have one of the lowest numbers of female participation in the workplace in Asia)—one can only hope that capitalism can finally work in favor of women so that when it comes to the commoditization of things, women are not on that list.

There's Something About Marriage

Why the Vote in Ireland Was Bad for Same-Sex Rights

Omar G. Encarnación

CATHAL MCNAUGHTON / REUTERS

People react as Ireland votes in favor of allowing same-sex marriage in a referendum, in Dublin May 23, 2015.

I n yet another example of the apparent paradox of Catholic nations leading the world on gay rights, Ireland, a quintessential Catholic society, has legalized same-sex marriage. Before Ireland, there was Uruguay, France, and Brazil (the world's largest

OMAR G. ENCARNACIÓN is Professor of Political Studies at Bard College and author Out in the Periphery: Latin America's Gay Rights Revolution, forthcoming from Oxford University Press.

Catholic nation as well as the largest same-sex marriage state) in 2013; Argentina and Portugal three years before that; and Spain, the country that inaugurated the trend of overwhelmingly Catholic nations legalizing same-sex marriage, five years before that.

When Spain's same-sex marriage law was enacted in 2005, only two other nations, the Netherlands and Belgium, had extended to same-sex couples the right to marry, with the Netherlands having done so only in 2001. As of now, and including Ireland, 19 countries protect that right. Of the almost 600 million people who today live in nations that allow same-sex marriage, more than 60 percent are in Catholic-majority nations—and that tally does not even include the "mini" state of Mexico City, a metropolis of some 20 million people, which legalized same-sex marriage in 2009, or Bolivia, Chile, Colombia, and Ecuador, which allow for same-sex civil unions with benefits that are very similar to marriage.

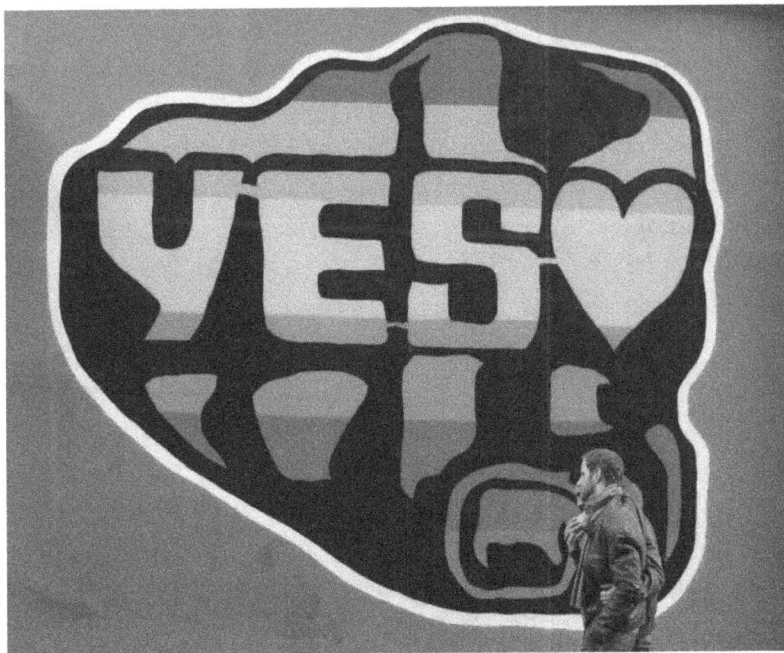

DARREN STAPLES / REUTERS

Men walk past Yes Campaign graffiti in central Dublin as Ireland holds a referendum on gay marriage, May 22, 2015.

To explain why Catholic-majority countries such as Ireland have embraced gay marriage, commentators have typically pointed to the decline of the Catholic Church's moral and political authority across the Catholic world. In Ireland, it came as a result of sex and child abuse scandals; in Spain and Latin America, because of the church's support of military regimes with reputations for wanton human rights abuses, including the disappearance of left-wing dissidents. But this is only part of the story. Polling data also suggest that Catholics, as a religious group, are more accepting of homosexuality than Protestants and Muslims.

According to Pew: "On average, Catholics are less morally opposed to abortion, homosexuality, artificial means of birth control, sex outside of marriage, divorce and drinking alcohol than are Protestants." It is further noted that: "The differences between Catholics and Protestants on most of these issues hold true even when accounting for levels of religious observance. For example, Protestants who participate in religious services at least once a week are somewhat more likely to oppose abortion and divorce—and considerably more likely to oppose homosexuality, sex outside of marriage and drinking alcohol—than are Catholics who attend Mass at least weekly." Certainly, it isn't unusual that an overwhelmingly Catholic country such as Ireland decided to back same-sex marriage.

What is unusual about Ireland, however, is the process through which the country settled the matter—not through the courts and the legislature, but via a national poll. In doing so, Ireland has claimed the title of the world's first country to gain same-sex marriage by popular demand. This is, arguably, a dubious honor. As I wrote in the pages of the *Irish Times,* "Although inspiring, Ireland's referendum is not a step forward for gay rights." There is, in fact, something unseemly about a nation putting the civil rights of a historically oppressed minority (it is worth remembering that homosexuality was regarded a crime in Ireland as recently as 1993) to a popular vote. Most civilized nations would never conceive of putting the rights of racial and ethnic minorities to a vote, so why should sexual minorities endure that indignity?

A CYNICAL HISTORY

No other country's experience best suggests the dark side of gay rights referendums than that of the United States, where foes of the gay community have perfected "letting the people decide" as a cynical tool for denying gay people their rights and for stopping the gay rights movement in its tracks. That ignominious experience goes all the way back to 1977, to the infamous Dade County, Florida, referendum on an ordinance passed by the county that banned discrimination on the basis of sexual orientation. Anita Bryant, a former beauty queen and spokeswoman for the Florida Citrus Commission (and hence Ms. Bryant's moniker as "the Orange Juice Queen"), spearheaded the referendum drive, which she ominously named the "Save Our Children" campaign. After a bitter political fight in which Bryant succeeded in depicting gays as pedophiles and predators, the repeal of the ordinance passed by almost 70 percent. The defeat encouraged groups in other cities (including St. Paul, Minnesota; Eugene, Oregon; and Wichita, Kansas) to overturn their own antidiscrimination ordinances, a major setback for the nascent gay rights movement.

By 2004, Republican operative Karl Rove cynically managed to put a same-sex marriage referendum on the ballot in ten states, including the all-important swing state of Ohio. He hoped to gin up support for George W. Bush's reelection campaign by motivating so-called value voters. The gay community was more than a little incensed at the idea that the public should have any say in whether or not a gay person could marry the person of his or her choosing. In subsequent years, that first wave of gay marriage referendums launched a tsunami of similar votes, with some of them, such as those of Texas and Virginia, so sweeping in their scope and mean-spirited in their purpose as to prevent the creation of domestic partnerships intended to grant same-sex couples hospital visitation rights. According to the gay rights lobby Human Rights Campaign, the nationwide average vote percentage for the 30 same-sex marriage referendums enacted in the United States since Alaska's ban was approved in 1998 is 67 to 33 percent, although in the South the average is considerably higher—75 to 22 percent.

Of all the same-sex marriage state bans implemented in the United States, the most heartbreaking (at least for the gay community) was California's Proposition 8 campaign, not least because it overturned an existing same-sex marriage law. But that was just the beginning. "Prop 8," scheduled to coincide with the 2008 presidential campaign, left in its wake a terrible legacy for the gay community, the state of California, and the United States as a whole—it defamed homosexuals as a menace to society and "worse than Germany's Third Reich," according to a Prop 8 coordinator; it left in legal limbo thousands of same-sex marriages; it tarnished the historical occasion of the United States having elected its first African American president.

Oddly enough, in an act of poetic justice, the victors in the Prop 8 fight have fared worst. After public opinion turned in favor of same-sex marriage, those who supported the referendum have found themselves fending off characterizations as retrogrades and bigots. Having lost the same-sex marriage war, the backers of Prop 8 are now demanding the right of florists, bakers, and photographers to refuse to provide their services to gay nuptials on the grounds that participation in such nuptials violates their deeply held religious beliefs. It's hard to see what good, if any, came from this sordid experience.

There is something unseemly about a nation putting the civil rights of a historically oppressed minority to a popular vote. Most civilized nations would never conceive of putting the rights of racial and ethnic minorities to a vote, so why should sexual minorities endure that indignity?

CONSTITUTIONAL UNCRISIS

The infamy that surrounds gay rights referendums begs the question of why the Irish would choose a popular poll to settle the issue of same-sex marriage. According to conventional wisdom, consulting the public on same-sex marriage was the only way to prevent same-sex marriage from being declared unconstitutional, since the constitution did not provide for same-sex marriage, a point that was stressed to me repeatedly by readers to my article in the *Irish Times*. I am not an expert on Irish constitutional law, but this reasoning strikes me as unconvincing. After all, Irish politicians had previously rejected a referendum on the issue because they feared it would prove too divisive, and instead decided to pass a same-sex civil unions law, enacted in 2011.

Moreover, it helps to think comparatively. In some countries, political leaders have deliberately refrained from allowing gay marriage referendums because they recognize that despite the appearance of being a democratic way to decide a contentious issue, gay rights referendums are actually demeaning to a democratic society. The most memorable example of a politician opposing such a vote on moral grounds is that of Argentine President Cristina Fernández de Kirchner. In 2010, she squelched any talk of a referendum on a same-sex marriage bill that was about to be debated by the Argentine National Congress. "It is unbecoming," she said, "of a democracy to put the rights of a minority to the whims of the majority." In the end, the Congress approved the bill.

At the same time, most states have legalized same-sex marriage without a provision in their constitution explicitly allowing them to do so. In fact, save for perhaps the Constitution of the Republic of South Africa, which was written after the dismantling of apartheid to ban virtually all kinds of discrimination, including discrimination based on sexual orientation, most of the world's constitutions do not envision same-sex marriage. Unsurprisingly, constitutional challenges to bills mandating same-sex marriages have become a matter of course in many countries, with all the ones of which I am aware unsuccessful.

The best-known case is Spain, where the 2005 same-sex marriage law survived a 2012 test by the Constitutional Tribunal. A conservative government had come into office pledging to overturn the law and arguing that it had "denaturalized" marriage as defined in the Spanish constitution as the union of a man and a woman. In the end, the tribunal refused to hear the appeal, leaving the same-sex law intact. In 2010, the Mexican Supreme Court reaffirmed as constitutional the legalization of same-sex marriage and adoption by Mexico City officials, after the conservative administration of Mexican President Vicente Fox initiated efforts to stop gay marriage in the Mexican capital on the grounds that the country's constitution does not allow it, which were subsequently picked up by President Felipe Calderón. Curiously, the Mexican justices cited American jurisprudence, especially *Loving v. Virginia,* the landmark case that ended the ban on interracial marriage in the United States, to justify their legal reasoning.

Just before France's 2013 same-sex marriage law went into effect, the law was blocked by a constitutional challenge from conservative legislators, but the country's highest judicial authority, the Constitutional Council, upheld the law, ruling that same-sex marriage "did not infringe on basic rights or liberties or national sovereignty." Conservative politicians in Brazil are currently challenging the Supreme Federal Court's 2011 decision that opened the way for same-sex marriage, arguing that the Brazilian constitution recognizes only heterosexual marriages. This challenge is not expected to go anywhere. In sum, it is not unthinkable that a same-sex marriage law in Ireland could have survived constitutional scrutiny, just as similar laws have in other countries.

In fairness to the Irish, one big difference between Ireland and Argentina, Mexico, and Spain is the liberalism of the courts. Largely because of the latter countries' recent experience with military dictatorship and the horrendous legacy of human rights abuses, the courts in Latin America and Spain have been extraordinarily receptive to arguments made by gay activists that "gay rights are human rights." Additionally, and also in contrast to Ireland, anticlericalism runs deep in the political culture of Latin America and Spain. Latin American politicians have eagerly embraced "marriage wars" to bash a once powerful Catholic establishment. Argentina's Kirchner took on Buenos Aires Archbishop

DANIEL AGUILAR / REUTERS

Temistocles (L) and his partner Daniel celebrate after getting married at the town hall in Mexico City March 11, 2010.

Jorge Mario Bergoglio (now Pope Francis) for his depiction of gay marriage as "an attack on God's plan and the devil's project." In a famous putdown, the president noted that Bergoglio's words were "reminiscent of the Inquisition."

After Cardinal Juan Sandoval Íñiguez, archbishop of Guadalajara, labeled the legalization of same-sex marriage and its adoption by Mexico City "an aberration" (he then asked, "Would you want to be adopted by a pair of faggots and lesbians?") and accused Mexico City Mayor Marcelo Ebrard of bribing the Supreme Court, Ebrard filed a defamation suit against the Catholic Church and chastised Íñiguez for failing to grasp that there is separation of church and state in Mexico: "We live in a secular state, and in it, whether we like it or not, the rule of law prevails; the Cardinal must obey the law like any other citizen of this country." The cardinal was censured by the Supreme Court in a unanimous decision supported even by the dissenting justices on the legalization of same-sex marriage.

FIGHTING IRISH

It seems that Irish politicians did not have the stomach for a political brawl and a protracted legal fight over same-sex marriage of the likes seen in Latin America and Spain and that they instead chose the least confrontational but most morally suspect path, which is understandable given Ireland's history of civil and political conflicts. Moreover, Ireland is a peculiar place, a point underscored by the fact that virtually the entire Irish political class was fully united behind the "Yes" campaign, making the outcome of the referendum certain, if not preordained. To their credit, those manning the "No" campaign resisted the temptation to demonize the gay community, which has not been the case in the United States. Actually, the losing side has been very gracious in accepting defeat. Signaling a willingness to reflect and move on, Dublin Archbishop and Primate of Ireland Diarmuid Martin noted that "we [the church] have to stop and have a reality check, not move into denial of realities."

All of this said, it is difficult to escape the conclusion that although things could have gone tragically wrong, things have instead played out very well in Ireland for the government, the LGBTQ community, and the nation as a whole. The triumph of the "Yes" campaign appears to be one not just for the gay community but for Ireland as a whole. Marriage equality is rightly held as a milestone in Irish history, a monumental achievement in the country's social and political development, and a repudiation of the Catholic Church's outmoded views on homosexuality. So we can rejoice in the outcome while decrying the process by which this outcome was attained. But just because the gay marriage referendum worked well for Ireland does not mean that it should be emulated by the rest of the world. Let us hope that Ireland's referendum is one example of settling gay rights that we will not see repeated anytime in the near future.

A Pain in the Athens

Why Greece Isn't to Blame for the Crisis

Mark Blyth

FRANCOIS LENOIR / REUTERS

A Greek flag flies behind a statue depicting the European unity outside the European Parliament ahead of a eurozone leaders summit on Greece in Brussels, Belgium, July 6, 2015.

W hen the anti-austerity party Syriza came to power in Greece in January 2015, Cornel Ban and I wrote in a *Foreign Affairs* article that, at some point, Europe was bound to face an Alexis Tsipras, the party's leader and Greek prime

---

MARK BLYTH is Eastman Professor of Political Economy at Brown University.

minister, "because there's only so long you can ask people to vote for impoverishment today based on promises of a better tomorrow that never arrives." Despite attempts by the eurogroup, the European Central Bank, and the International Monetary Fund since February 2015 to harangue Greece into ever more austerity, the Greeks voted by an even bigger margin than they voted for Syriza to say "no" once more. So the score is now democracy 2, austerity 0. But now what? To answer that question, we need to be clear about what this crisis is and what it is not. Surprisingly, despite endless lazy moralizing commentary to the contrary, Greece has very little to do with the crisis that bears its name. To see why, it is best to follow the money—and those who bank it.

The roots of the crisis lie far away from Greece; they lie in the architecture of European banking. When the euro came into existence in 1999, not only did the Greeks get to borrow like the Germans, everyone's banks got to borrow and lend in what was effectively a cheap foreign currency. And with super-low rates,

FRANCOIS LENOIR / REUTERS

Greece's Prime Minister Alexis Tsipras arrives at an emergency eurozone summit in Brussels, Belgium, July 7, 2015.

countries clamoring to get into the euro, and a continent-wide credit boom underway, it made sense for national banks to expand private lending as far as the euro could reach.

So European banks' asset footprints (loans and other assets) expanded massively throughout the first decade of the euro, especially into the European periphery. Indeed, according the Bank of International Settlements, by 2010 when the crisis hit, French banks held the equivalent of nearly 465 billion euros in so-called impaired periphery assets, while German banks had 493 billion on their books. Only a small part of those impaired assets were Greek, and here's the rub: Greece made up two percent of the eurozone in 2010, and Greece's revised budget deficit that year was 15 percent of the country's GDP—that's 0.3 percent of the eurozone's economy. In other words, the Greek deficit was a rounding error, not a reason to panic. Unless, of course, the folks holding Greek debts, those big banks in the eurozone core, had, over the prior decade, grown to twice the size (in terms of assets) of—and with operational leverage ratios (assets divided by liabilities) twice as high as—their "too big to fail" American counterparts, which they had done. In such an over-levered world, if Greece defaulted, those banks would need to sell other similar sovereign assets to cover the losses. But all those sell contracts hitting the market at once would trigger a bank run throughout the bond markets of the eurozone that could wipe out core European banks.

Clearly something had to be done to stop the rot, and that something was the troika program for Greece, which succeeded in stopping the bond market bank run—keeping the Greeks in and the yields down—at the cost of making a quarter of Greeks unemployed and destroying nearly a third of the country's GDP. Consequently, Greece is now just 1.7 percent of the eurozone, and the standoff of the past few months has been over tax and spending mixes of a few billion euros. Why, then, was there no deal for Greece, especially when the IMF's own research has said that these policies are at best counterproductive, and how has such a small economy managed to generate such a mortal threat to the euro?

Part of the story, as we wrote in January, was the political risk that Syriza presented, which threatened to embolden other anti-creditor coalitions across Europe, such as Podemos in Spain. But another part lay in what the European elites buried deep within their supposed bailouts for Greece. Namely, the bailouts weren't for Greece at all. They were bailouts-on-the-quiet for Europe's big banks, and taxpayers in core countries are now being stuck with the bill since the Greeks have refused to pay. It is this hidden game that lies at the heart of Greece's decision to say "no" and Europe's inability to solve the problem.

Greece was given two bailouts. The first lasted from May 2010 through June 2013 and consisted of a 30 billion euro–Stand By Agreement from the IMF and 80 billion euro in bilateral loans from other EU governments. The second lasted from 2012 until the end of 2014 (in practice, it lasted until a few days ago) and comprised another 19.8 billion euro from the IMF and another 144.7 billion euro disbursed from an entity set up in late 2010 called the

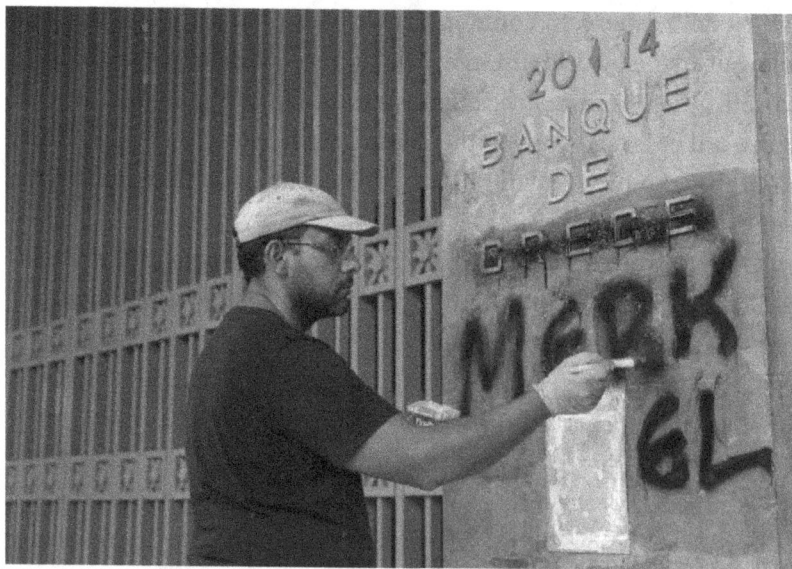

YANNIS BEHRAKIS / REUTERS

A worker cleans graffiti outside the central Bank of Greece building in Athens, Greece, July 7, 2015.

European Financial Stability Facility (EFSF, now the European Stability Mechanism, ESM). Not all of these funds were disbursed. The final figure "loaned" to Greece was around 230 billion euro.

The EFSF was a company the EU set up in Luxemburg "to preserve financial stability in Europe's economic and monetary union" by issuing bonds to the tune of 440 billion euro that would generate loans to countries in trouble. So what did they do with that funding? They raised bonds to bail Greece's creditors—the banks of France and Germany mainly—via loans to Greece. Greece was thus a mere conduit for a bailout. It was not a recipient in any significant way, despite what is constantly repeated in the media. Of the roughly 230 billion euro disbursed to Greece, it is estimated that only 27 billion went toward keeping the Greek state running. Indeed, by 2013 Greece was running a surplus and did not need such financing. Accordingly, 65 percent of the loans to Greece went straight through Greece to core banks for interest payments, maturing debt, and for domestic bank recapitalization demanded by the lenders. By another accounting, 90 percent of the "loans to Greece" bypassed Greece entirely.

Telling though those numbers are, they still miss the fact that, after Mario Draghi took over from Jean Claude Trichet at the ECB in late 2011, Draghi dumped around 1.2 trillion euro of public money into the European banking system to bring down yields in the Long Term Refinancing Operations (LTROs). Bond yields went down and bond prices soon went up. This delighted bondholders, who got to sell their now LTRO-boosted bonds back to the governments that had just bailed them out. In March 2012, the Greek government, under the auspices of the troika, launched a buy-back scheme that bought out creditors, private and national central banks, at a 53.4 percent discount to the face value of the bond. In doing so, 164 billion euro of debt was handed over from the private sector to the EFSF. That debt now sits in the successor facility to the EFSF, the European Stability Mechanism, where it causes much instability. So if we want to understand why the combined powers of the eurozone can't deal with a problem the size of a U.S. defense contract overrun, it's probably wise to start here and not with corrupt Greeks or Swabian housewives' financial wisdom. As former Bundesbank Chief Karl Otto Pöhl admitted, the whole shebang "was about protecting German banks, but especially the French banks, from debt write-offs."

Think about it this way. If 230 billion euro had been given to Greece, it would have amounted to just under 21,000 euros per person. Given such largess, it would have been impossible to generate a 25 percent unemployment rate among adults, over 50 percent unemployment among youth, a sharp increase in elderly poverty, and a near collapse of the banking system—even with the troika's austerity package in place.

To fix the problem, someone in core Europe is going to have to own up to all of the above and admit that their money wasn't given to lazy Greeks but to already-bailed bankers who, despite a face-value haircut, ended up making a profit on the deal. Doing so would, however, also entail admitting that by shifting, quite deliberately, responsibility from reckless lenders to irresponsible (national) borrowers, Europe regenerated exactly the type of petty nationalism, in which moral Germans face off against corrupt Greeks, that the EU was designed to eliminate. And owning up to that, especially when mainstream parties' vote shares are dwindling and parties such as Syriza are ascendant, simply isn't going to happen. So what is?

Despite Germany being a serial defaulter that received debt relief four times in the twentieth century, Chancellor Angela Merkel is not about to cop to bailing out D-Bank and pinning it on the Greeks. Neither is French President Francois Hollande or anyone else. In short, the possibilities for a sensible solution are fading by the day, and the inevitability of Grexit looms large. It is telling that Tsipras and his colleagues repeatedly used the phrase "48 hours"—sometimes "72 hours"—as the deadline for getting a new deal with creditors once the vote was in. This number referred to how long Greek banks could probably stay solvent once the score went to 2-0.

At the time of writing, the ECB is not only violating its own statutes by limiting emergency liquidity assistance to Greek banks, but is also raising the haircuts on Greek collateral offered for new cash. In other words, the ECB, far from being an independent central bank, is acting as the eurogroup's enforcer, despite the risk that doing so poses to the European project as a whole. We've never understood Greece because we have refused to see the crisis for what it was—a continuation of a series of bailouts for the financial sector that started in 2008 and that rumbles on today. It's so much easier to blame the Greeks and then be surprised when they refuse to play along with the script.

Enlightened Despots, Then and Now

The Truth About an Islamic Enlightenment

John M. Owen IV and J. Judd Owen

A man fixes a mosque's minaret with a crescent moon symbol in Jeddah, July 6, 2015.

JOHN M. OWEN is Taylor Professor of Politics at the University of Virginia and author of *Confronting Political Islam: Six Lessons from the West's Past* (Princeton University Press, 2015).

J. JUDD OWEN is Associate Professor of Political Science at Emory University and author of *Making Religion Safe for Democracy: Transformation from Hobbes to Tocqueville* (Cambridge University Press, 2015).

By now, the pattern is predictable. Jihadists carry out a suicide bombing, a ritual beheading, an immolation, a murder in a Western city, or some other such barbarism, and newspapers, magazines, and blogs demand or suggest an Islamic enlightenment. By "enlightenment," they generally mean the turn that the West took centuries ago from faith to reason, from religion to science, from traditional authority to democracy, and from religious violence to tolerance: in short, modernity. Before the Enlightenment, European and American Christians burned witches and heretics and fought and died for obscure otherworldly beliefs; after the Enlightenment, they did not. And so, the argument goes, Islamic societies need their own enlightenment to wrest them back to the future.

Setting aside that the Enlightenment did not end violence and self-destruction in the West (see: World War I, fascism, World War II, and the Cold War), calls for enlightenment in the Islamic world typically fail to recognize a few vital facts, not least of which is that Islamic societies have been grappling for generations with the Enlightenment, both the West's and their own. Indeed, the very turmoil and violence that are thrashing Muslim societies are in no small measure a reaction against the forces of enlightenment, rather than a sign that those forces await initiation. The West's own history shows that the Enlightenment was not an event but a long, tumultuous, and often bloody struggle, one that remains deeply (although less horrifically) contentious to this day.

> The Enlightenment, then, in both the natural and political sciences, set itself against traditional authorities, particularly the church and the state it sanctioned.

The Enlightenment, then, in both the natural and political sciences, set itself against traditional authorities, particularly the church and the state it sanctioned. To succeed, the new learning required political support, which it found most importantly in monarchs who wanted to continue to weaken the two entities that blocked their ambitions: the Church and the aristocracy. The

Enlightenment provided these ambitious kings with various justifications and opportunities.

In 1651, Thomas Hobbes published *Leviathan*, a masterful Enlightenment case for absolute monarchy based, paradoxically, on the assertion of natural individual rights. In the spirit of modern physics, Hobbes reduced human beings to material bodies and was unambiguous about the need to tame religious institutions by making the head of the essentially secular state the supreme authority over religion. The enlightened sovereign would support the useful sciences with a view to material security and prosperity, while

The frontispiece of the book Leviathan by Thomas Hobbes; engraving by Abraham Bosse, 1650.

reforming legal and religious education with a view to enlightening the people. Enlightenment would operate from the top down, and would be compatible with the suppression of dangerous (especially seditious religious) teachings.

Enlightenment political philosophers were united in their embrace of the new science and their opposition to the old order, but many parted ways with Hobbes' enlightened absolutism, pushing instead for republican or democratic government with more expansive individual freedoms—in other words, the liberal democracy that most associate with the Enlightenment today. But it is important to bear in mind that the Western Enlightenment contained both absolutist and democratic strands.

Indeed, the century that followed Hobbes, the heyday of Enlightenment philosophy and science, is often known as the era of enlightened absolutism. Frederick the Great of Prussia, an ardent admirer and associate of the French Enlightenment philosopher Voltaire, set the pace, sponsoring modern science and applying its findings to agriculture, transportation, government, and (not least) war-making. Monarchs in Austria, Denmark, France, Russia, Spain, and Sweden, among others, followed Frederick's example. These countries were far from democratic. Indeed, thanks in part to their ability to harness Enlightenment techniques for state organization, their rulers enjoyed much more power than their medieval counterparts ever did.

It wasn't until the revolutions of the late eighteenth century in North America, France, the Netherlands, and Poland (ruled by Russia and Prussia) that enlightened absolutism gave way to the alternative republican or democratic strand of the Enlightenment. But that transition itself entailed catastrophic violence within and among states. As the historian R. R. Palmer has written, the republican revolutions began as an aristocratic reaction against monarchs and the war debts they had accumulated on the back of the new technology. As landed elites began to assert their old rights and privileges, impoverished common people turned on their enlightened despots. (Neither the king of England nor the Dutch stadtholder qualified as an enlightened absolutist, but even they were following the general trend toward centralizing power.) European monarchs turned on the Enlightenment once the French Revolution inspired rebellion throughout the continent, which spiraled into terror and foreign wars in 1792–93. Out of those traumas emerged Napoleon, the Enlightenment on horseback, whose struggle against Europe's monarchs—now zealous converts to traditionalism—thrust Europe into the longest and most destructive wars it had seen in 150 years.

It was Napoleon who, with his invasion of Ottoman-ruled Egypt in 1798, first brought the modern Enlightenment into the Muslim world.

Napoleon's aggressive Enlightenment Empire brings us to the Islamic world. For it was Napoleon who, with his invasion of Ottoman-ruled Egypt in 1798, first brought the modern Enlightenment into the Muslim world. Napoleon introduced the printing press and founded an academy of sciences (the Institut d'Égypte, which was severely damaged during the popular uprising of 2011). Here, the phrase "modern Enlightenment" is key; during the Middle Ages, Islamic philosophers had already spearheaded a quite different enlightenment by introducing ancient Greek philosophy and science into Islamic tradition. By way of Muslim-ruled Spain, this medieval rationalism profoundly influenced Christian and Jewish thought for centuries to come. But that original Islamic Enlightenment had lain dormant for centuries by the time Bonaparte arrived.

In the wake of Napoleon's withdrawal in 1801, the Ottoman Empire proved unable to reestablish control and, under the strong 43-year rule of Muhammad Ali, Egypt began a process of modernization. In the nineteenth century, many Ottoman elites—soldiers, bureaucrats, educators—likewise found the principles of modern practical learning appealing, even though those principles had come from the same Europe that was humiliating their once-mighty empire. By the end of the century, the Young Turks saw traditional Islam's domination of law, state, and learning as the primary source of Muslim weakness, and the adoption of Enlightenment technology, beliefs, and practices as the surest route to ending their humiliation. A decisive moment came in 1924, when Mustafa Kemal

Ataturk dissolved the Ottoman caliphate, founded the Republic of Turkey, and put the secular state decisively in charge of religion. "We do not consider our principles as dogmas contained in books that are said to come from heaven. We derive our inspiration not from heaven, or from an unseen world, but directly from life," Ataturk said in 1937. His words would have pleased Thomas Hobbes.

As Frederick the Great had done in eighteenth-century Europe, Atatürk inspired imitators in the Muslim world: Reza Shah in Iran, Muhammad Ali Jinnah in Pakistan, Gamal Abdel Nasser in Egypt, the Baathists in Syria and Iraq. These were no backward-looking traditionalists. They were forward-looking state builders seeking to apply modern rationality and science to society. But like the enlightened absolutists of eighteenth-century Europe, twentieth-century secular Muslim rulers were power-seekers. The Ataturks and Nassers needed to improve the lot of the common people in order to win them over and weaken the authority of traditional religious

WIKIMEDIA

Mustafa Kemal Bey (Ataturk) with an Ottoman military officer and Bedouin forces in Derna, Tripolitania Vilayet, 1912.

teaching and institutions. They were authoritarian not in spite of Enlightenment influence but because of it.

Much has happened in the Middle East since the heady days of mid-twentieth-century secularism. Traditional Islam never went away, and it continued to be used to back monarchical rule in Saudi Arabia and elsewhere. It evolved into modern Islamism, in all its variety, and established regimes in Iran and Sudan. Secular regimes in Egypt, Syria, Iraq, Pakistan, and elsewhere found that they had to Islamicize to varying degrees just to maintain their legitimacy.

There is no question that, today, Islamism is resurgent, with a radicalized wing growing in militancy and brutality. But Westerners should not be fooled by the strength of Islamism into thinking that the Muslim world simply needs a modern enlightenment. The violence that continues to shake so many Muslim societies is in part about Islam's ongoing confrontation with an enlightenment imposed on Muslim societies from above, much as European absolute monarchs imposed the young Western Enlightenment on their societies centuries ago. Whatever the future may hold for an Islamic enlightenment, we should understand that, like its Western precursor, its progress is bound to be violent precisely because it is both a spiritual and a political project that is bound to generate both religious and political reactions. Indeed, if we want to see what the early phases of the West's own Enlightenment looked like, we could do worse than to look at today's Middle East.

Muslims have encountered post-Enlightenment Western society in myriad ways for a long time, and they are torn among themselves in reaction. Today's Islamists, whose reaction understandably preoccupies us, do not live in a historical bubble. Indeed, more than a few of those rallying to the cause spent their formative years in Western societies and were educated in Western schools. They have seen the West's version of the future and do not believe that it works. Not only, then, does the West's past help us understand Islamism today, Islam's present is also instructive about where the West finds itself in the long, turbulent, and still ongoing history of its own Enlightenment.

Putin's Syria Strategy

Russian Airstrikes and What Comes Next

Dmitry Adamsky

A Sukhoi Su-30SM jet fighter flies above a kite during an airshow outside Moscow, August 29, 2015.

As some had predicted, in late September Russia intervened in Syria. In Moscow's eyes, the move reconfirmed Russia's status as an indispensable power and broke down its international isolation by diverting attention from Ukraine, winning

DMITRY ADAMSKY is Associate Professor, School of Government, and Institute for Policy and Strategy, at IDC Herzliya.

some applause in the EU and possibly creating conditions for sanctions relief. Most important, the United States softened its position on Syrian President Bashar al-Assad, whose resignation is no longer considered a precondition for settlement.

To examine what Moscow is ultimately after—its theory of victory—and how it will get there, one has to make some assumptions. First, disputes about Russian President Vladimir Putin's prudence and the Kremlin's aptitude for sound national security policy are unsettled. But empirical evidence suggests that Putin, though not necessarily a chess grandmaster, does have his own systematic method for managing crises and strategic interactions. He is guided by his understanding of Russia's past and his deeply held visions of its future. Not infallible, he nonetheless examines his options, changes course in response to events, and demonstrates a judoka's aptitude for improvisation and exploitation of his adversaries' mistakes.

Second, the desired endgame for Moscow is presumably a stabilized Syria through which Russia can preserve its regional presence. Initially, Moscow will try to secure and strengthen its stronghold on Syria's coast—in the Latakia and Tartus facilities, where it has long maintained a presence. Russia could expand its beachhead by increasing airfield capacity and equipping its docks for bigger battle and transport ships. Russia would use its optimized launching pad to supply Assad's and its own forces in their battle to stabilize and protect the borders of "little Syria," the regime's current strongholds. Meanwhile, Moscow may start to inch toward a political settlement. The Kremlin will likely first push for the restoration of Syria's prewar borders. If that seems infeasible or too risky, though, it may be satisfied with the little Syria borders. Although Moscow's preference will be for Assad to stay in control in both scenarios, it would not likely stand in the way of replacing him as long as the new government would protect Moscow's interests and enable its regional power projection.

Third, Moscow probably understands that its position in Syria is hardly strong and that intervention may become a fiasco. It is aware of U.S. regional misadventures and its own in Afghanistan,

Russian Foreign Minister Sergei Lavrov and U.S. Secretary of State John Kerry speak to the media regarding the situation in Syria, September 30, 2015.

the North Caucasus, and Ukraine. If judged by Russian military and area studies periodicals of recent years, Russian experts and strategists have a clear picture of best and worst practices during military interventions and air campaigns, although the extent to which such knowledge will translate into policy is unclear.

Strategically, Russian expert commentary has zeroed in on the limits of Russia's vast military capacity against an ideological enemy. Brute force can inflict heavy blows on jihadist fighters but not on Salafist ideas. And so strategists have debated just how to wage the battle in Syria and the appropriate risks to take on and costs to pay. Moscow is mindful of the potential difficulties of sustaining public tolerance for a war in a distant country, particularly as Russia's economy declines and the hostilities in Donbass continue. Finally, the Kremlin is sensitive to concerns of business elites about the prudence of the move, especially the potential parallels to Russia's misadventures in Afghanistan.

With all that could go wrong, Putin's decision to intervene was probably fraught. Wary of overextension, the Kremlin must be trying to find the exact right balance between under- and over-shooting. Here, the Kremlin is likely to adopt an approach that corresponds with the Soviet principle of reasonable sufficiency. First articulated by Soviet leader Mikhail Gorbachev, the principle originally meant fielding only the military force necessary to protect against outside threats. Applied to the Syrian context, the principle may mean limiting the scale of intervention to the minimum level that would still allow Russia to project influence in Syria. In Ukraine, Moscow learned hard lessons about the limits of force—additional military involvement has not enabled it to settle the situation in Donbass once and for all. Indeed, it has only drawn Russia further into a battle it neither expected nor desired. This time, reasonable sufficiency may prevent Moscow from crossing the culminating point of intervention—the moment after which additional application of force becomes counterproductive.

INTERVENTION TACTICS

In its intervention in Syria, Moscow has sought the broadest possible alliance. Even so, the military core of the coalition is quite narrow: Assad's remaining units, Iranian Revolutionary Guard and Basij forces, Hezbollah, and the Iraqi government.

In this campaign, Moscow will likely try to design and oversee coalition operations and act as a force multiplier on the frontlines. In addition to diplomatic support, Russia may provide planning and logistical assistance; command, control communication, and intelligence capabilities; and of course air support. The air component of the mission could perhaps include fighter-bombers, close support jets, combat and transport helicopters, and drones—all of which would be deployed to back up the pro-Assad forces. Russia may use its interdiction jets to deter possible air strikes on Assad-controlled ground and field surface-to-air systems and advanced jets for the defense of all expeditionary components.

At the same time, in keeping with the principle of reasonable sufficiency, Moscow will likely delegate most ground warfare to its allies. It could participate in operational planning, share visual and signal intelligence, and designate targets. But it seems unlikely that battalions of Russian troops will become a regular site in Damascus. Instead, Moscow is likely to boost its programs to train and advise Assad's units, which it views and presents, for political and military reasons, as the most effective battlefield force against ISIS.

Moscow might be confident that it can design an effective coalition campaign, building on its experiences from dozens of exercises conducted with Collective Security Treaty and Shanghai Cooperation Organizations. Even so, it is likely to be concerned about coalition forces' interoperability. To be sure, on the strategic level, Iran, Russia, and Syria, and possibly Hezbollah and Iraq, have reportedly coordinated on some military efforts since summer. Moscow is familiar with Syrian forces, which it trained, equipped, and educated for decades, while Assad has deep experience with Hezbollah. And both countries have cooperated with Iran. But the group doesn't have much experience working together as a whole, and

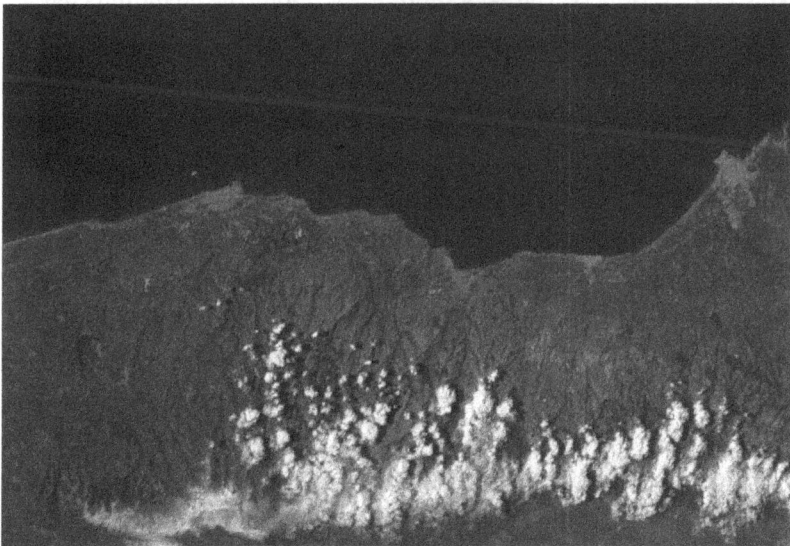

REUTERS

Latakia (R) and Tartus, two coastal towns in Syria, are pictured in this handout photo courtesy of Col. Chris Hadfield of the Canadian Space Agency, March 20, 2013.

most of the parties have never conducted large-scale coalition operations before.

Russia's ability to coordinate its partners' activities will be key. According to Russian commentators, ISIS's success mostly derives from Assad's inability to concentrate his military's efforts against the group, from the previous coalition's half-measures, and from the lack of coordination among the rebels. By bringing some focus and rationality to the anti-ISIS campaign, the Russian-led coalition seeks to reverse the course of the war. Given existing Russian military theory, the air campaign is likely to take the form of strikes on the three systems holding ISIS together: the chain of command and control, supply chains, and economic centers of gravity. As air strikes try to fragment ISIS, ground operations will seek to dismantle small local groups of fighters. The campaign doesn't need to be large scale, it just needs to reverse current trends, demonstrate the strength of the incumbent regime, and facilitate conditions for a political process.

In some aspects, the campaign design may also draw from Russia's New Generation Warfare—a set of ideas about the changing character of war that has been circulating in the Russian strategic community under the current chief of the general staff, Valery Gerasimov. This notion already shaped the 2014 Russian military doctrine and subsequent operations in Ukraine. The concept minimizes the role of large-scale military operations of the industrial war era and instead combines hard and soft power across military, diplomatic, and economic domains. It capitalizes on indirect action, informational operations, paramilitaries, and special operation forces backed by sophisticated military capabilities. Done right, the concept naturally corresponds with the principle of reasonable sufficiency.

In this case, Moscow might minimize its visible presence, blurring, for domestic and international purposes, the line between involvement and intervention. This doesn't mean, of course, that Russia will send no operatives into the fray of the ground warfare. Indeed, if the "little green man" ("polite people," in the Russian parlance) of the Russian armed forces, together with Donbass field commanders and pro-Russian Chechen fighters start appearing on the Syrian battlefields, it should come as no surprise. Unlike in Donbass or Crimea, these fighters will have more issues with blending in. Given their experience and training, though, they can still act as a force multiplier. And if Russia deploys them while keeping mindful of reasonable sufficiency, it can hope to avoid a quagmire in Syria along the lines of the one in Donbass and achieve something closer to the effective campaign in Crimea.

ALL FOR ONE?

Making waves is easier than controlling them. For Moscow, the main risk in Syria is overextension. During the initial surge against ISIS, the coalition is likely to rally around their common goal. But as the campaign wears on, and especially if situation in the Assad-held parts of Syria stabilizes, the interests of coalition members may diverge. Iran and Syria may seek to take the battle further eastward and northward, hoping to fully restore Syria to Assad.

MAXIM ZMEYEV / REUTERS

Syria's ambassador to Russia Riad Haddad speaks during a news conference in Moscow, October 1, 2015.

Moscow may have more limited goals and will seek to switch to settlement and stabilization as soon as possible. If Moscow is unable to facilitate a political solution and cannot impose its will on its allies, they may drag Russia deeper into fighting. The same may occur if the campaign, for whatever reason, does not progress as planned and demands more investment. The Kremlin probably realizes that its Shia coalition with Assad, Iran, Hezbollah, and Iraq may galvanize the Sunnis against them, even precipitating an alliance of ISIS and other radical armed groups. The risk is all the greater given that Moscow does not differentiate between moderate and extremist rebels and qualifies any anti-Assad combatants as terrorists—as the targets of strikes to date make clear.

The second risk is related to Israel. Jerusalem is likely to stand firm against any game-changing weapons transfers to Hezbollah, and it will not tolerate fighting spilling over its borders. Knowing this, Hezbollah, Iran, and Assad may be planning to operate within Russian areas of responsibility and as close as possible to Russian forces, turning them into human shields. Israel has routinely been conducting strikes exactly where the Russians are now expanding their foothold. Recent talks between Putin and Israeli Prime Minister Benjamin Netanyahu on deconflicting their air, naval, and electromagnetic operations will only partially address the issue. If the tail wags the dog, Moscow and Jerusalem will face hard choices. Israel has signaled its neutrality toward the conflict, but it is unclear how the Israeli Air Force will tolerate potential jamming, cyber-strikes, and limits of its space for maneuvering or if Moscow decides to establish an electromagnetic *cordon sanitaire* and anti access-area denial sphere around the pro-Assad coalition's operational theater.

Finally, Moscow understands that there will be a persistent threat of homegrown radicalization. It knows that its activities in Syria could instigate hatred among its large Sunni population and further motivate jihadists to bring their fight back to the Russian heartland, the North Caucasus, and Central Asia. The radicalization of Muslim conscripts within the Russian military is already a concern for Moscow—and things could get much worse.

Even if Moscow is aware of the dangers and wants to avoid the culminating point of intervention, it is unclear whether the current campaign in Syria will go as smoothly as Russia thinks. Still, it is worth keeping in mind an old adage: Russia is never as strong as it seems and is never as weak as it appears.

All in Good FON

Why Freedom of Navigation Is Business as Usual in the South China Sea

Mira Rapp-Hooper

U.S. President Barack Obama and Chinese President Xi Jinping depart at the conclusion of a joint news conference in the Rose Garden, September 25, 2015.

B y all appearances, the U.S. Navy is poised to begin Freedom of Navigation exercises in the South China Sea. Rumors first emerged in May 2015 that the Pentagon was

MIRA RAPP-HOOPER is a Senior Fellow in the Asia-Pacific Security Program at the Center for a New American Security.

contemplating military operations around China's new artificial islands among the Spratly Islands. Through such exercises, the United States would aim to demonstrate that it does not recognize spurious Chinese claims to water and airspace around the islands. So far, the Department of Defense has declined to make moves near China's so-called Great Wall of Sand. The administration has, however, consistently stated that there are U.S. national interests in freedom of navigation and overflight in this vital waterway, where $5 trillion of global trade passes each year. With the presidential summit between U.S. President Barack Obama and Chinese President Xi Jinping now complete, operations seem imminent.

At the very least, the public debate about South China Sea Freedom of Navigation Operations (FONOPS) has already begun. Already, two myths about their role in U.S. foreign policy have emerged. The first is that they are a strict alternative to diplomacy with China. According to a Politico article, this narrative holds that there are some "military leaders who want to exercise their freedom of navigation" while diplomats are demurring in the interest of continued diplomacy with China. The second misconception is that they would challenge China's claims to territory in the Spratly Islands. Even the best reporting on these exercises suggests, as did a recent *Wall Street Journal* article, that the purpose of FONOPS is to "directly contest Chinese territorial claims."

Combined, these two misconceptions suggest that U.S. FONOPS would be a serious escalation by Washington in the South China Sea. As the history of the Freedom of Navigation Program and its relationship to international law make clear, however, such operations would complement U.S. diplomacy and, although they would contest China's claims to water and airspace under the UN Convention on the Law of the Sea (UNCLOS), they would not contest its claims to territory. If the Obama administration decides to begin these exercises in the coming days, there are a few ways for it to signal that FONOPS are simply business as usual.

DAVID GRAY / REUTERS

Commander of the U.S. Pacific Fleet Admiral Scott Swift stands in front of a large poster of an Australian Navy frigate as he prepares to hold a media conference at the 2015 Pacific International Maratime Exposition in Sydney, Australia, October 6, 2015. In a strongly worded address, Swift said the United States remained "as committed as ever" to protect freedom of navigation through the region.

REPUTATION FOR FON

Freedom of navigation operations have long been a part of U.S. foreign policy. In 1801–1805, an embryonic U.S. Navy saw its first action protecting American overseas commercial interests in the Barbary Wars, when pirates demanded that the Jefferson administration pay tribute so that merchant ships could pass through the Mediterranean Sea. It was not until 1979, however, under U.S. President Jimmy Carter, that the mission was formalized into a freedom of navigation program. The U.S. FON program was developed in conjunction with UNCLOS and was officially established a year later. Although Washington is not a signatory to UNCLOS, the goal of the FON program has always been to promote international adherence to it. The FON program does so by challenging "excessive claims" to maritime and air space that do not conform with the convention.

The Department of State and Department of Defense jointly oversee the FON program, which has three major components. The State Department files diplomatic protests of excessive claims; State and Defense consult with their international counterparts on claims' consistency with international law and work with the through military-to-military engagements; and Defense conducts what it calls "operational assertions," through which it demonstrates physically the United States' nonrecognition of excessive claims.

Although there is no open source repository of data on the exact frequency and location of the Pentagon's FONOPS, available figures indicate that the United States uses the tool quite frequently, particularly in Asia. The Department of Defense challenged 19 excessive claims worldwide in 2013 and 35 claims in 2014. Of those 35, 19 were located in the U.S. Pacific Command's geographic region of responsibility. And they were equal opportunity challenges; in 2013–2014, the Department conducted FONOPS of various forms against China, Malaysia, the Philippines, Taiwan, and Vietnam—each of the countries that occupies territory in the South China Sea.

Despite these facts, the debate in Washington has persisted in the idea that FONOPS are extraordinary measures above and beyond diplomacy. Reports have suggested that U.S. military commanders support South China Sea FONOPS, whereas the White House and the Pentagon have been hesitant to pursue them. Others have argued that the Obama administration has preferred the State Department's "creative diplomacy" to the use of FONOPS, suggesting that there is room for only one agency or approach to engaging China's island building in the South China Sea. But diplomacy and FONOPS are complementary tools, not stark alternatives, and a decision to begin FONOPS should not be seen as a victory for military over civilian leaders, or as a sign that diplomatic efforts have been exhausted.

For their part, Chinese officials have stated that they would interpret U.S. exercises within 12 nautical miles of the features they

RITCHIE B. TONGO / REUTERS

The alleged ongoing land reclamation by China at Subi reef in the Spratlys group of islands in the South China Sea, May 11, 2015.

hold in the Spratlys as provocative challenges to Chinese sovereignty. Beijing has every reason to imply that it would respond harshly to any maneuvers. The trouble is that the same misconception about the purpose of FONOPS has been proffered in Washington as well.

In a recent Senate hearing, Senator John McCain (R-Ariz.) argued that Washington's failure to transit within 12 nautical miles of China's claims "grants de facto recognition" of them. A report soon followed with the headline "McCain: U.S. Should Ignore China's Claims in South China Sea." This was likely not the message the Senator intended to convey, but reporting has consistently suggested that FONOPS would be used to push back against China's claims to territory. The United States, however, has a long-standing policy that it does not take a position on other countries' sovereignty disputes. FONOPS are meant to challenge excessive claims to water and airspace; they do not challenge territorial claims.

In other words, the FONOPS reality is both considerably more nuanced and far less escalatory than the popular narrative suggests.

FON WITH OBAMA

In the aftermath of the Obama-Xi summit and with Beijing firmly committed to its position that it will continue to build what it likes in the Spratly Islands, Washington may begin FONOPS in the area in the coming days or weeks. If it does so, the basic facts of the Freedom of Navigation Program and of UNCLOS should serve as reminders that these operations do not represent a significant change in U.S. policy in the South China Sea.

First, under UNCLOS' principle of innocent passage, foreign navies are entitled to transit within a state's 12-nautical-mile territorial sea, as long as that vessel does nothing that is prejudicial to peace. Put differently, even if the United States didrecognize China's sovereignty in the Spratlys, which it does not, international law permits it to pass peacefully nearby. China exercised this right in early September, when it transited U.S. territorial waters in the Bering Sea. The International Court of Justice has affirmed that this and operations like FONOPS are consistent with the right of innocent passage.

Second, precisely because the South China Sea territories are disputed, and because Washington does not take a position on such sovereignty disputes, it need not recognize territorial seas or airspace around any of China's artificial features—or those of any other countries. In short, territorial seas are a function of recognized state sovereignty, and where that sovereignty is disputed, vessels and aircraft may pass freely.

Third, even if China's Spratly holdings were uncontested, the fact remains that Beijing's seven island features are artificial. Under UNCLOS, man-made islands do not confer territorial seas or airspace. Rather, they are granted only a 500-meter safety zone. In China's case, before its building spree, at least three of its seven artificial islands were low-tide elevations or reefs, rather than rocks or islands. Under international law, these features are not even subject to sovereignty claims—by China, or by anyone else. By this logic, even without persistent sovereignty disputes, Mischief Reef, Gaven Reef, and Subi Reef would not be entitled to water or

Policemen stand guard behind placards during a rally against China's behavior in the disputed islands in the South China Sea, in front of the Chinese Consulate in Makati, Manila, August 31, 2015.

airspace of their own, and therefore may be especially appropriate features around which to transit.

As Washington prepares to conduct FONOPS, there are two steps it can take to show that these exercises are not escalatory but are usual practice in the global commons. First, Washington should alert countries in the region about its plans and should ask for their public support where possible. Australia, India, and Japan have all recently expressed serious concern that China's island building will threaten freedom of navigation in the South China Sea. Their public support for U.S. maneuvers would demonstrate that this is not an issue of U.S.-Chinese tit-for-tat but a matter of regional diplomacy and rule of law.

Second, whether the Pentagon decides to operate within 12 nautical miles of only those Chinese features that were previously reefs, or opts to transit near other Chinese artificial islands too, it should conduct FONOPS around other claimants' features as well, including low-lying reefs that are controlled by the Philippines or rocks held by Malaysia or Vietnam. Given that these countries are themselves gravely concerned about freedom of navigation and have expressed a willingness to sign on to recent U.S. diplomatic proposals to halt destabilizing activities in the South China Sea, it is unlikely that they would object to inclusion in this demonstration of legal principle.

U.S. Secretary of Defense Ashton Carter declared in May that the United States would continue to "fly, sail, and operate wherever international law allows," and the Obama administration reiterated this pledge to Xi in September. Spratly Islands FONOPS are entirely consistent with this position. By soliciting the support of other regional states and conducting exercises around the features of multiple claimants, Washington can reinforce this program's long history and record. Freedom of navigation is just business as usual in the South China Sea.

www.ingramcontent.com/pod-product-compliance
Lightning Source LLC
Chambersburg PA
CBHW062216270326
41930CB00009B/1754